private places

private places

judith wilson

photography by **frederic vasseur**

HD

HARPER
DESIGN

An Imprint of HarperCollins*Publishers*

PRIVATE PLACES
Text copyright © Judith Wilson 2005
Design and photographs © Jacqui Small 2005

First published in 2005 by Harper Design,
An Imprint of HarperCollins*Publishers*
10 East 53rd Street, New York, NY 10022
Tel: (212) 207-7000; Fax: (212) 207-7654
HarperDesign@harpercollins.com; www.harpercollins.com

HarperCollins books may be purchased for educational, business, or
sales promotional use. For information, please write: Special Markets
Department, HarperCollins Publishers Inc., 10 East 53rd Street,
New York, NY 10022.

Library of Congress Control Number: 2004114515

ISBN: 0-06-072354-8

Printed in Singapore
First Printing, 2005

contents

introduction

A private place should be planned in minute detail. Remember that you can be as self-indulgent as you like—after all, it's your space.

We live in a frantic world. In the twenty-first century, everyday activities and their accompanying pressures are almost non-stop. Whatever life stage we are at, there are demands on time and heavy schedules—for work, leisure, and socializing. And with today's sophisticated communication systems, we're expected to be on call 24/7. It's a noisy world, too. Unless we live deep in the countryside, few of us escape the hum of unseen road traffic, the ring of the phone, or the buzz of electronic gadgets. It's human nature to adapt, but often it's at the cost of a tranquil domestic environment.

In addition, contemporary living trends conspire against the search for old-fashioned peace and quiet. We don't all live in vast lofts; nevertheless, many of us have become obsessed with the Holy Grail of an open-plan living environment. Whatever the property type—from a narrow townhouse to a city apartment—its walls are knocked down with enthusiasm, all the better to create big, airy, multifunctional spaces for everyone to share. And "everyone" is the key word. Family units are becoming more fluid—extra stepchildren or elderly relatives may share the home for some or all of the time. Formal entertaining has largely been replaced by casual drop-in social events. Many houses also boast a home office, with assorted daily workers coming in and out. It's no wonder we find it hard to establish quiet places of our own.

LEFT **Devising a room to look tranquil, with simple lines and a cool, neutral color scheme, is one way to create a peaceful haven at home. Just one or two focal points—a great view from the window or an exuberant vase of flowers—will help counteract the stimuli of a busy day.**

THIS PAGE **Resolve** to have at least one private zone in your home and tailor its furniture arrangement and color scheme according to your notion of tranquility. In this lateral space, the bed is snugly cloistered behind a wall partition, while the eau de nil and white color palette promotes a serene mood.

OPPOSITE PAGE **Space** isn't the issue: a private place may be shoehorned into the tiniest of areas. What matters most is that the retreat is minutely planned to deliver uninterrupted time out in a busy home. This peaceful reading nook has been slotted below a double-height entrance-hall ceiling.

Interior design and architecture trends also encourage us to pursue individual activities en masse. The giant kitchen table, or island unit, is specifically designed so that one person can cook, the kids can eat, and someone else can work on a laptop, all at the same time. The double-height living space is championed as sociable and multifunctional. And because the cell phone is so mobile, there's no excuse to hide away for a quiet conversation. All the things we used to value as solitary pursuits, from letter writing to working a crossword puzzle, have been dragged into the public arena. Multitasking has its benefits, but somewhere along the line we've forgotten that we need time to be private.

From a young age, children are taught to respect no-go areas at home or at school, or to leave people alone if asked to, and will retreat to their bedrooms. But as adults, we find it hard to assert our right to some privacy. We're also steeped in a culture that celebrates doing things in public. You can't turn on the television without seeing reality programs spying on other people's lives. The notion of privacy has all but slipped from view.

Instead we're all reminded—by media and marketing executives alike—that life is frenetic, and that to counteract it, we should chill out and slow down at spas, boutique hotels, and yoga retreats. It's appealing once in a while, but expensive and time consuming in the long term. Plus, you still have to share those spaces with other people. All that relaxation is lost if, once home again, you're cast straight back into a noisy living space. There's no point lighting a scented candle if there isn't a tranquil escape.

With that in mind, it makes sense to turn attention back to home. The pleasure of a pure white bathroom designed to maximize relaxation, or a book-lined study, can provide untold tranquility and pleasure. Depending on the size of available living space, plans can be grand or ultra simple (usually the best solution—think of a monk's cell). Even in a tiny space, there is potential to be exploited.

What matters most, before taking plans further, is to crystallize your personal notion of a private place. Think through your lifestyle at home. Who lives there on a regular basis? Who feels the need for privacy? (Not everyone does—some thrive on being at the center of the action.) The *Oxford English Dictionary* defines privacy as "being alone and undisturbed." For some, that will also include being quiet, away from television and conversation. For others, being alone isn't essential—they may happily share a study with a partner. But knowing exactly which individuals are likely to enter a designated private zone certainly is. Consider the purpose of having a private place: is it for a specific activity or for quiet contemplation? Only once you have answered that question will you be able to create the right environment.

Early on, it helps to make a distinction between establishing privacy from visitors and the need for an occasional retreat from family members at home. Sort the former first. Most of us are naturally sociable and love to entertain friends at home. We know that guests won't barge into the master bedroom's bathroom or start rummaging in the study. But if it's a busy household—with teenagers or a home office or live-in household help—boundaries must be clearly delineated. Once privacy is 100 percent assured, so is relaxation.

So look at your home with fresh eyes and mentally divide the layout into "public" and "private" areas. Public spaces include the hall, kitchen, formal entertaining rooms such as a living room or dining room, a downstairs powder room (or an upstairs family bathroom), plus the yard and access to it. Visitors might comfortably be expected to stray into any of these areas. (And, by convention, we tend to put most time and money into decorating such common spaces.) Private rooms—the bedrooms, bathrooms, a study or a family room, and any stairs or corridors leading to them—must be protected.

Figure out whether simple, subtle changes can be used to separate off-limits rooms. The alterations might involve adding physical divisions or changes in layout. In a single-level apartment, for example, entertaining rooms can be divided from a bedroom corridor by adding sand-blasted sliding doors or inserting a series of narrow double doors, creating the impression of an enfilade of inner rooms. In a townhouse, a bedroom on

OPPOSITE PAGE, TOP **If you are devising a personal corner just for you, take time to get the detailing right. Fill bookshelves with favorite reading material located at a user-friendly height for easy browsing. The shape of the chair is all-important—low-slung and comfy is best.**

OPPOSITE PAGE, BOTTOM **A well-managed color scheme, which deliberately switches from bold colors in a busy traffic area to soothing shades in a relaxation zone, can help differentiate between public and private areas. In this upstairs living room, pale stone, bleached wood, glass, and taupe shades are calming choices.**

LEFT **In an open-plan space, it's still possible to create clear divisions between public and private zones. This cozy, book-lined sitting area is set apart from the busy hall, home study, and kitchen space using a cubic book case, as well as contrasting wall colors, which provide a subtle sense of separation.**

the quieter, more private upstairs floor may be converted into a secluded sitting room, reserving the downstairs drawing room for entertaining. In an urban loft, the addition of solid partition walls will make a crucial distinction.

Solutions may be more radical. If guests regularly have to troop upstairs to the family bathroom, bite the financial bullet and install a downstairs powder room. If you have a live-in nanny, site her room on the ground floor and install a shower room in the basement, well away from family bedrooms and bathrooms. A home office will seem less exposed to family members if there's separate access at the side of the house or via a basement. For those with money to invest, there's the option of adding an extension to a house, converting an attic, or constructing a study at the end of the garden for a truly custommade space.

Creating a bolthole within the family home is vital, too. We all need time out from our favorite people (as they do from us). In an ideal world at home, each adult would have a study or workroom, with children's bedrooms doubling as theirs. But if space doesn't permit that, then resolve to create at least one peaceful zone. Set the ground rules, and make sure that everyone knows the room is for chilling out. It's worth considering that a study has reverse potential. If there's one particularly noisy family member (who likes loud music or computer games, for example), it's to everybody's benefit to allocate them a room of their own. A study is like an adult playroom: messes don't need to be cleared up and the door can be shut at the end of the day.

It goes without saying that a private place should be planned in minute detail. Remember that you can be as self-indulgent as you like—after all, it's your space. If there is a sewing room, plan customized shelving to hold boxes of fabrics; if it's a sitting room devoted to music, add ceiling speakers, plenty of CDs, and a deep, comfortable sofa. Be individual with a decorative scheme. Too often we agonize over the "right" colors and fabrics to put in our public rooms lest friends and guests criticize our taste. A private space, on the other hand, can be as bright or as fantastical as we choose. Consider whether this is a place to be shared with special people. If so, include a visiting chair and make the approach to the room (or outdoor retreat) just a little bit mysterious.

Above all, a private place must have soul. It should be a retreat that can soothe, a space that inspires, a comfort zone that offers peace and quiet, day or night. And to that end, as well as providing the means to talk on the phone, write, read, or engage in other solitary pursuits, it must offer somewhere to sit—or preferably lie. We live in a busy world, but we all deserve a place where we can switch off and dream, or simply stare at a single imaginary bright spot on the wall.

ABOVE **An outside area—a patio, balcony, or tiny city yard—can be a particularly soothing place to retreat to. Pick a spot that affords good natural views—even if there's no garden, look for treetops or a slice of sky—and preferably well-sheltered, so it can be used year round.**

RIGHT **Keep ambience uppermost in your mind when you're planning a private retreat. Harness natural "props"—daylight filtered through blinds, the waft of a breeze from open windows or a ceiling fan, or the sound of garden birdsong— and only the simplest of decorative treatments will be required.**

room retreats

We expect home to be a private place. We relish shutting the front door and retreating from the outside world. For some, just to surround themselves again with familiar things is the signal to start the process of relaxation, but many of us require an extra boost. It's not enough to choose a home that has an inherent ambience, a natural good feeling; we need to consciously create rooms that are peaceful places to be.

Not every room in the house can offer the promise of sanctuary. For a start, every home has its hub of activity, in and out of which family members, friends, and visitors constantly revolve. These days, that key zone is often the kitchen, source of food, sociability, and entertainment. Other busy areas will often include the hall, a playroom, a family room, and so on. It would be unrealistic to expect these hard-working, high-traffic spaces to be soothing or to afford us personal privacy in a busy household.

Instead, concentrate on rooms that really can be reclaimed as your own. In a larger house, that may mean the opportunity to have a study, a grown-up sitting room, or a peaceful private bathroom. But even in a compact home, it's possible to make your bedroom a retreat, or to decorate a communal sitting room or bathroom to calm everyone and provide quiet nooks for rest and relaxation.

serene
sitting rooms

Even if there's an open-plan living area on the ground floor, try to assign one room as a separate sitting room.

These days we've almost lost sight of the restrained and tranquil sitting room, with a solitary clock marking the time and soothing vistas of green. Either sofas and chairs have been swallowed up into an open-plan living area, leaving no opportunity for privacy, or a separate sitting room is dominated by the TV and, increasingly, the computer as well. While it's impossible to mourn the passing of the formal drawing room or parlor (full of uncomfortable chairs), there is still a need for a soothing sitting room at home. A good one should offer solace at the end of a busy day and physical separation from kitchen-life in a hectic household.

So even if there's an open-plan living area on the ground floor, try to assign one room as a separate sitting room. In many homes, it has been the practice to have a grown-up drawing room in the biggest entertaining space and a small family "den." Think about reversing that trend. Isn't it better to relegate the TV and computer to a large multifunctional kitchen/sitting/dining area and reserve a small room as a peaceful sanctum? Size is not the issue: this is not a room for impressing guests, but a retreat to please you. To ensure maximum peace (and privacy), it's a good idea to choose an upstairs room that's close to the bedrooms, or one to the rear of a single-level apartment.

Early on, define the purpose of the sitting room. We all have a different notion of a serene space. It could be the chance to replace the TV with a hi-tech music system with "invisible" ceiling speakers.

PREVIOUS PAGE **A quiet spot boasting a dining table clustered with comfortable chairs is a tranquil place to relax. Close to big windows, yet furnished with dramatic pendant lighting, such a retreat works well by day and night.**

LEFT **Despite its modest proportions, this sitting room feels peaceful, not cramped. Well-edited furniture and accessories make the difference: an L-shaped modular sofa, a piece of art, and a low coffee table keep things simple.**

For some, it gives license to line the room with shelves of books and magazines; for others, a tranquil sitting room is a minimalist's dream—all empty walls and cool colors, with zero reminders of everyday paperwork. In an adults-only sitting room opening onto an enclosed garden, you can focus on lying down and contemplating the natural world. Think carefully before installing a computer, and ask yourself whether a phone is truly necessary. If this is a chill-out room, then it's okay to remove communications so that everyone can (literally) switch off.

When getting the orientation of the room right, remember that a sitting room planned for contemplation, rather than socializing, requires a different set of criteria. Most of us don't have the luxury of choosing between multiple reception rooms, but try to remain open-minded while you mentally review the available space across the whole house or apartment. Formal drawing rooms are often at the front of a property and may boast elaborate architectural detailing, higher ceilings, and more generous dimensions. A soothing sitting room, on the other hand, will benefit from more intimate proportions, so you might consider converting a bedroom. The room should be as peaceful as possible, so may be better situated at the rear of the house. While the ideal formal sitting room faces south, a west-facing room also has many benefits: evening sunshine and shadows fluttering across bare walls are remarkably atmospheric.

Good windows are crucial. Conventionally, we rate them in terms of size (and how much light they let in) and architectural style (grand or simple). Yet in a room devoted to relaxation, the view beyond the window is vital.

ABOVE LEFT **In this new house there was the luxury to locate a sitting room next to the garden. Large windows and a simple interior enhance the rural views.**

ABOVE RIGHT **This sitting room is expertly planned to cater to quiet contemplation and reading. Floor-to-ceiling shelves flank two walls, and there's a good mix of lighting.**

RIGHT **The comfortable, low-slung upholstery is good-looking and practical—even lying down, you can see out of the window. Plenty of side tables keep drinks and books close at hand.**

Lighting has become a powerful mood-inducing tool, so take time to plan it.

THIS PAGE **This sitting room delivers a unified visual statement—romantic, contemporary, and peaceful. Well-conceived task and overhead lighting play up the modern and period style mix.**

OPPOSITE PAGE **The relaxed mood of this room is achieved partly by careful integration of all services. Heating is via a floor-mounted cylinder radiator, while lighting is a floor lamp scaled-up to suit the room's dimensions.**

There's no point lying on a daybed if there's a vista of a brick wall. In an ideal world, of course, the best views are of countryside, the sea, or a garden. If you're lucky enough to have such a view, then arrange the furniture (or at least one chair) to maximize such glimpses. For inner-city dwellers, remember there is real beauty to be found in an urban view, especially at night with car taillights or half-illuminated skyscrapers. For most of us, stuck with more prosaic street views, the answer may be to put shutters on the lower section of windows or replace clear glass with acid-etched glass panes. That way, the eye is directed upward to prettier views of sky or treetops.

First thoughts should be devoted to getting the "skin" of the room just right. That means hiding all wiring, gas pipes, and technology, and—because some of these can be seamlessly concealed within cupboards and shelves—devising storage, too. Many of the best ambience-inducing features in a modern-day sitting room come with a raft of complex wiring, so decide now what is required and where. Think not only of lighting—a tricky enough issue in itself—but of whether there's a place for a gas real-flame fire. For some, a relaxing sitting room will also mean including a sophisticated home-entertainment system (including music, DVDs, and a plasma screen). These days there are specialized companies who plan and install them and who will be able to offer advice on concealing the technology.

Lighting is now so sophisticated that it has become a powerful mood-inducing tool, so take time to plan it. There is such a vast choice available that it's important to do some research. Visit specialized shops, and if there is a free consulting service, use it. Employing a freelance lighting designer can also be a worthwhile investment. In a room devoted to relaxation, it's

not essential to install ceiling lights (if there are existing fixtures, at least add a dimmer switch). Instead, concentrate on mood-inducing decorative lights, from LED wall lamps to under-shelf fiber-optic illumination. Add a selection of task lights—good options include a floor lamp, clip-on light, and a gooseneck-style desk lamp—which can be moved around the room to suit different chairs. Choose a minimum of 60-watt bulbs to ensure good reading light.

Inevitably, choice of color will have a powerful impact on ambience. We all have a different emotional response to color, but certain shades are fail-safe for creating tranquility. White, of course, is popular and the ultimate choice for Zenlike calm. It works especially well in a room surrounded by outdoor greenery. If pure white seems too stark, then investigate the many variegated tones leading from white: stone, dove gray, off-white, bone, and blue-toned ice-whites. If more defined color appeals, sludgy pastel tones make a good choice. (Avoid pure, saturated shades, though, as they are stimulating, not peaceful.) Excellent off-pastels to try include lichen gray, gray-blue, and mushroom pink, or experiment with clearer pale pastels such as lilac or eau de nil. Don't be afraid to use dark shades: charcoal gray or deep biscuit, for example, can create a very soothing interior.

Resolve to make the process of choosing paint colors fun, not stressful. Many of us, faced with a sitting room to decorate, swing wildly from picking a fail-safe neutral (intended to please everyone) to formal traditional wallpaper, thinking this is the "right" choice for a grown-up room. The proper answer is to choose a wall color that genuinely makes the sitting room occupants feel good. So take a lateral approach. Long before scrutinizing paint color samples, gather magazine tear-sheets, fabric

LEFT **This sanctuary of a sitting room proves that a pure white scheme and modern furniture can still look cozy. The sociable U-shaped furniture arrangement, the intimate corner lighting, and the organic curve of the table help soften the look and mood.**

ABOVE **Temper pure white with a judicious choice of textures. In this small sitting room, gently crumpled white cotton covers and cushions, teamed with a gray cashmere throw, prevent the room from looking clinical.**

RIGHT **Off-whites, cream, biscuit, or soft grays make a soothing tonal statement in a traditional interior, as they team well with natural surfaces, from bleached floorboards to stone. In this room, pink peonies help "lift" the monochromatic scheme.**

OPPOSITE PAGE **A fire—whether real or gas "real flame"—creates an instant focal point in a sitting room and decoration and furniture layout should be planned accordingly. In this cool blue-gray room, a pedestal table with a slim silhouette and a low stool have been deliberately chosen so as not to impede the view of the fireplace. A comforting beanbag and another low chair have been casually placed on each side, making it easy to draw close to the fire.**

LEFT **Despite the austerity of the plain stone fireplace and painted floorboards, this sitting room has a luxurious, relaxed mood. The natural textures of the logs are enhanced with a fluffy rug, squishy denim beanbag, and the glow of the flames.**

BELOW **A generous expanse of open-plan shelving, a deep leather chair, and an open fireplace make this sitting-room niche the obvious place to curl up with a good book.**

swatches, or pieces of clothing in shades that naturally appeal. Lay them out on the floor. Isolate the one the eyes travel toward first. Only then is it the right moment to find a paint sample to match.

It goes without saying that an open fire provides instant ambience, so try to include one. Nothing beats the smell, crackle, and visual appeal of a real fire, and some find the ritual of cleaning, laying, and lighting as relaxing as the dancing flame itself. If an open fire isn't possible, then a gas "real-flame" fire is an excellent second best. To focus attention on the flames, pick a simple surround: in a minimally-styled room, a hole-in-the-wall feature is preferable. Even if there is a mantelpiece, try to avoid the temptation to clutter up the top with too many photos and ornaments.

Beautiful, well-thought-out storage goes a very long way to promoting tranquility. No one can relax properly if the place isn't neat, or if shelves bulge uncomfortably. But we all have a different threshold for clutter.

Before investing in new cabinets, decide how important it is for the sitting room to be mess-free. Be honest: if relaxation truly means indulging in bare walls, then plan extra storage for all the other rooms, and relocate all the books, videos, and photo albums conventionally kept in the sitting room. If it's acceptable to include wall storage, what type is best? A wall of open-plan shelving, kept painstakingly well ordered, will appeal to those who want books and CDs on hand. Others will prefer floor-to-ceiling wall cupboards for stashing clutter, with flush doors in wood veneer, sand-blasted glass, or composite board painted to match the wall color.

When choosing fabrics for a decorative scheme, we often latch first onto the color and pattern of a given textile. A patterned fabric is an effective design shorthand: consciously or unconsciously, we will pick a floral chintz to label a sitting room as formal or a designer abstract to define a modern look. But in the serene sitting room, fabrics should fulfill a different role. Try to stick to plain materials, perhaps with a single accent pattern. Then concentrate on choosing tactile upholstery, in the anticipation that there will be as much relaxing as possible! Pure linen and linen-cotton blends feel deliciously cool to the touch and look fresh. But a heavier weight and sensual velvet, 100 percent wool, and chenille are good choices, too. Exploit the fact that this is a private sitting room. It's okay to pick self-indulgent pale colors, safe in the knowledge that upholstery is unlikely to be ruined by party guests.

As for window treatments, use fabric as a tool to manipulate ambience. Pick textiles that drape well if used unlined, to give a soft and informal look and so that sunlight will filter through prettily. Linen, raw silk, and taffeta are all excellent sophisticated choices, while cotton, lawn, hemp, and muslin are cheaper and more relaxed options. A good floaty texture is essential, so that when windows are open, curtains will billow

gently in the breeze. Likewise, an unlined blind will cut out the glare of direct sunlight while still allowing adequate daylight into the room. Window treatments are also vital for keeping a room private. We would all like a sitting room free from prying eyes, so that we can enjoy sunsets or a clear starry sky from the comfort of the sofa without the need for pulling down the blinds. In reality, some form of screening is often essential. Wood Venetian blinds and plantation shutters are flexible options, as they can be adjusted to let in lots of light while maintaining privacy. Plain or hole-punched white roll-up shades are a cheaper alternative, as are very fine voile or natural linen Swedish-style roll-up blinds. If you prefer the softer outline of a curtain, unlined linen tie-top curtains screen effectively.

Pick furniture for a serene sitting room with a sassy spirit of self-indulgence. Interior designers and architects are fond of telling us to plan a sitting room with the comfort of others (that is, guests and visitors)

OPPOSITE PAGE, LEFT **Off-whites and creams are serene-looking color choices for fabric; a mix of textures creates visual interest. A combination of heavyweight linen and sheers adds moody ambience to this room as it filters the light.**

OPPOSITE PAGE, RIGHT **Here, luxurious fabric is combined with deep-buttoned upholstery to create an indulgent mood. At the window, stainless-steel mesh panels backed with violet taffeta enhance pretty shadows.**

ABOVE LEFT **Think beyond conventional blinds and curtains for dramatic-looking window treatments, particularly if the room needs permanent screening. In this sitting room, the bay window has pivoting shutters, with sheers made from a high-tech structural fabric.**

ABOVE RIGHT **In a high-rise apartment, when privacy isn't an issue, enhance a fabulous view by abstaining from window treatments entirely.**

foremost in our minds. They admonish that there should be space for people to move easily around, spare tables for drinks, and a flexible furniture arrangement so that the room can be quickly cleared for a party. In the sitting room planned as a retreat, you can afford to be a little more selfish. Of course, comfortable seating remains a priority—and friends aren't banned entirely—but tailor it to the needs of the family first.

Identify favored relaxation styles. Who likes to curl up, sprawl out, or simply lie down? Pick furniture styles accordingly. With high backs and straight sides, a traditional Knole sofa or a contemporary take on a wing chair is ideal for reading. Every sitting room should have a daybed or sofa long enough to lie down on. Make sure it is placed directly under a window (for a sky view) and furnish with a generous bolster or several fat cushions to prop up on while reading. An upholstered footstool or two positively encourages occupants to put their feet up.

Whether it's entirely reserved for chilling out or is a place for quiet, intimate entertaining, the serene sitting room needs at least a few accessories. How many, and of what type, will depend on the decorative style. As a rule of thumb, it is always more relaxing to be in a room furnished in a restrained manner—with a few really beautiful pieces of art on the wall, a well-filled glass vase of fresh flowers, and a cluster of family photographs, for example—so keep to favorite things that have a meaning and that please the senses.

ABOVE LEFT **Upholstered furniture should be deep enough for curling up, and the sofa long enough to sprawl on. It pays to invest in good upholstery— cushions should be plump and retain their shape.**

ABOVE RIGHT **You are aiming for a sitting room that is soothing, but not bland, so it's vital to include a decorative focus. In this large warehouse space, a colorful handprinted wall-hung textile creates simple yet strong drama.**

THIS PAGE **Pick adaptable furniture, in styles that can be adjusted to different ways of relaxing. In this sitting room, the contemporary Knole-style sofa has sides that may be lowered for reclining, while the low-slung retro armchair swivels.**

Identify favored relaxation styles. Who likes to curl up, sprawl out, or simply lie down? Pick furniture styles accordingly.

In today's space-compromised living spaces, a study seems a self-indulgent extra. But don't we all dream of having a room of our own?

The "home office"—whether we actively work from home or not—has all but taken the place of what is more traditionally known as the study. That's a pity, as the two are very different rooms with very different functions. In a typical home office, technology dominates: the computer and printer take center stage, paired with filing cabinets and an office chair. Very rarely is there any attempt at creating ambience. Neither is this a room generally considered to be private. An adult in search of a few minutes' peace and quiet is as likely to find a child playing computer games in here as space to relax and write a letter.

A study, on the other hand, positively bristles with good associations. We think of a shady, welcoming room, often book-lined, always snug, with favorite books, papers, and music tucked away and perhaps a cozy armchair in the corner. It is a room actively designed to feel womblike. There's a natural assumption that a study is a room for just one, plus the occasional visitor, in a pinch. Whether it's called a writing room, a study, or a den, it's considered a bolthole for solitary pursuits, such as reading, thinking, or quiet contemplation.

In today's space-compromised living spaces, a study seems a self-indulgent extra. But don't we all dream of having a room of our own? Before you conclude that you don't have a free room, why not take a moment to consider if a designated study is possible by reviewing all rooms in the house?

RIGHT **A study needn't be a serious space—it might be a practical workroom, devoted to sewing or painting, or a specialized zone, such as a photography darkroom. Decorate it with a practical, freestanding, yet whimsical touch, so a little light chaos looks charming, rather than a mess.**

sanctuary
studies

Could you relocate a table and chairs to the kitchen in order to free up a little-used dining room, for example? How many spare bedrooms are there? If guests are infrequent, is each one really necessary? It may be a better use of space to invest in a sofabed for the occasional stopover and turn a spare bedroom into a study. Be imaginative. In an older property, there may be an odd little space—a walk-in closet or a discarded pantry—that could be cleverly adapted into a scaled-down den. In new houses, the smallest bedroom is often barely big enough for a single bed. Why not buy the kids bunk beds and commandeer that tiny bedroom as your own?

It is location, not size, that creates a successful study. Small can feel more intimate and there's less chance of another adult trying to squeeze in a second desk. First, try to find a room at home that is in a quiet spot. Everyone has an individual noise threshold (and some can work only in total silence), but no one wants to hear a TV through the walls. Ideal location also depends on when the study will be used and for what. For those studying by day, a ground-floor room is best, so that it's possible to switch off from work at night. In a family house where there are young children with early

OPPOSITE PAGE **If it's impossible to dedicate a entire room to a study, section off a portion of the living room. Use deep, moody colors, book-lined walls, and comfy sofas to mark it out as a cozy den.**

ABOVE LEFT **The tiniest bedroom can be converted into a study. This one maximizes floor space by centrally siting the desk, while an entire wall is devoted to storage. The plain-painted cupboard doors, adorned with a dried leaf, prevent the books from overpowering the room.**

ABOVE RIGHT **A retreat intended for correspondence needs only a desk and chair, so it can easily be squeezed into the corner of a larger room.**

bedtimes, an upstairs room close to the bedrooms is fine for evening study. It's trickier to find peace among a number of adults, so grab anywhere away from the main living areas—a small room off a landing or a converted attic, perhaps. Digging out the basement to create an entirely new floor is an increasingly popular option if your budget permits.

If noise and interruption are big issues, it's also worth considering the location. If your study is too close to the hall, you will be expected to answer the door, and arriving and departing visitors will be an annoyance. Too high up the house (in the attic, say), and it's vital to include an entry system so that you can open the front door without budging. How close is the nearest bathroom? And how far is it to the coffeemaker? Indulging in a study might mean including a mini fridge and a coffeepot. Mentally check through other potential household noises. A study next to the laundry room may seem like a great idea until the hum of the dryer intrudes.

Once it has been decided to have a study, define if anyone else is allowed to share. Two adults in a family house will get plenty of peace and quiet, as it's unlikely that both will want to be in there at the same time. One person who works at home and another who commutes to work, wanting to use the study only for evening relaxation, can happily share, for example. However tiny the space, try to avoid desk-sharing, as most individuals are ridiculously territorial about desk space. If it's likely that there will be arguments about each other's mess of papers, then plan for separate desks and

LEFT **When sharing a study, make it a rule to keep the work surface uncluttered, then locate storage at the rear, so that neither of you need view the other's filing.**

ABOVE **Attics make great studies, as they are physically far from household noise. They may also have the benefit of large roof windows, so they can make a particularly good choice for a sewing room or an artist's studio, where it is vital to have plenty of natural light.**

RIGHT **For busy couples, a twin study—with facing desks—can be an ideal solution for enjoying shared, but quiet, times at home. If the room is to be used for activity rather than contemplation, choose an energizing, clean-cut decorative scheme.**

Most individuals are ridiculously territorial about desk space, so plan for separate desks and sets of stationery.

LEFT **If your budget won't stretch to expensive custom-made storage, select the simplest off-the-peg shelving system you can find, and repeat it across an entire wall. A simple design of open cubes looks smart, and will neatly hold everything from books to stacked CDs or files.**

OPPOSITE PAGE, LEFT **It's tempting to cram filing cabinets beneath the desk top, but in a confined space this can look clumsy, as well as restricting leg room. Keep the desk area unimpeded, and either wall-mount storage or align a bank of filing cabinets on an adjacent wall.**

OPPOSITE PAGE, RIGHT **Remember to plan storage to cater for smaller bits and pieces, such as stationery, as well as including larger-scale bookcases. Rattan baskets work well here, but you could also consider fabric-covered boxes or metal tins.**

sets of stationery. If not, consider choosing a wide desktop, furnished with two chairs, so partners can work side by side.

The whole point of a study is that it is devoted to quiet activity. While traditionally we associate it with intellectual pursuits, from serious reading to studying, these days it might also be a tranquil place for perching with the laptop, surfing the Web, doing the Internet shopping, or emailing friends well away from the envious gaze of children, who'd prefer to be burning a CD. It might be the place to watch a solitary DVD or practice daily meditation, or it might be a workroom for sewing. For the media obsessed, it can be a room for catching up on satellite news no one else wants to watch. So before starting to furnish and plan the room, get clear in your own mind what activities and pursuits the study is catering to.

Creating a study is exciting, because it's a one-off chance to design a truly individual environment. Once gained, don't take this precious small room for granted. Too often, the study becomes a dumping ground for shabby furniture unsuitable for "public" rooms, or for unfiled family paperwork. Even worse, there's often an unwillingness to invest in a room that visitors aren't going to see. Take the opposite view. Money spent on creating good-quality (and adequate) storage, an inviting décor, and pretty furniture will make a study's occupant very happy indeed. Precisely because a special room is private, it should be a place where you lavish plenty of time and attention.

It's not essential for every study to be book lined, but it certainly raises the atmosphere, and imposes a subtle form of soundproofing. Try to have at least one wall of floor-to-ceiling shelves. Built-in shelves are expensive, but usually the best solution. They needn't be exclusively for books, but can house an archive LP collection, or include segregated niches for DVDs, magazines, or photograph albums. In a tiny room, storage must work particularly hard, so it pays to measure books, CDs, and so on to make sure they fit perfectly onto each shelf. Alternatively, shelves can be

designed with an adjustable racking system. Include deep shelves at a low level, fitted with open wicker baskets, or fabric-covered boxes that cater for inevitable bits and pieces.

If a wall of shelving feels overpowering, design it to rise from floor to tabletop height, then continue from shoulder height to the ceiling. The resulting mid-level worktop is a good place to keep filing trays, which otherwise clutter up a desk. In a particularly tiny room, design shelves to include a built-in worktop—with a niche below for the office chair and a filing cabinet on castors. When designing built-in shelving, think decorative, not utilitarian. Composite shelves painted to match the walls or finished in a rich-looking wood veneer look more inviting than cheap (and weak) laminate shelving units from the home improvement store.

Freestanding storage also has its place. The occasional office-style piece—a filing cabinet, a multidrawer stationery unit, a traditional architect's filing chest—can be immensely useful. The latter has huge potential, keeping in order everything from wrapping paper to the children's artwork. With the advent of the home office, many designer and chain stores have good-looking cabinets in chic colors, or you can visit second-hand office supply stores. But mix utility pieces with decorative furniture, from a retro office chair to a newly upholstered Victorian slipper chair. The aim is to create an inviting room, rather than a formal office.

When it comes to choosing key activity pieces—including a desk and a chair—consider personal comfort and good looks as well as practicality.

ABOVE **This tiny study has a flip-down worktop and ample ceiling cupboards, yet folds away to nothing. It's a space-saving solution if the study doubles as a spare bedroom.**

RIGHT **Add colorful decorative touches to distinguish a home study from a work office. A bright cushion, or a repaint in a fun color, will personalize an old piece of office furniture.**

OPPOSITE PAGE **It's possible to edit down key pieces to a desk (provided it has ample drawer storage), swivel chair, and efficient desk lamp.**

ABOVE LEFT **Use furniture and accessories to personalize your study, so that even if storage is functional and equipment ergonomic it's a space you feel relaxed in, too. In this pristine white office, the quirky lamp and pictures add character.**

ABOVE RIGHT **If space is tight, just a few square yards of an open-plan space may be pressed into service. Choose adaptable furniture so the study area is easily cleared.**

OPPOSITE PAGE **If this is a study for music or film appreciation, plan for related equipment, and consider building in the essentials—from a wall-mounted plasma screen to the stereo. Don't forget customized shelving.**

also with an adjustable arm, is a better choice than a standing lamp, which has a limited pool of light. Clip-on spotlights can be easily attached to a nearby bookshelf and moved around to suit several different chairs. Install overhead lighting in the form of low-voltage downlights and add a dimmer switch; on winter evenings it's useful to have general illumination as well as task lighting to make the study an inviting place to be.

If there's no chance of a separate study, then it's comparatively easy to add a discreet desk and chair to a sitting room or even a bedroom. Choice of furniture is vital since it must blend well with everything else. In a classical room, consider using a traditional bureau with pull-down flap or a console table. But even a wooden worktop, built into a chimneypiece alcove, can provide a few square feet of privacy. Look for furniture with drawers so that all paperwork can be stowed away easily, and consider a lock for at least some drawers so private papers remain exactly that. Finally, make sure that there's space to tuck away the chair—preferably beneath the desk top—so it won't impede human traffic flow when not in use.

tranquil
bedrooms

Above all, the bedroom must deliver ultimate peace and comfort so a good night's rest is assured.

The bedroom plays a unique and sensitive role in our daily home life. It is the place where we start the day, sliding from unconsciousness to an alert state, so it can have a powerful impact on our mood. Likewise, it's where we seek to relax after a hectic schedule, composing our minds before bed. It must be a practical place to cater to all those inevitable short bursts of activity, from getting dressed or exercising before work to sorting the laundry or post-bath pampering. Above all, it is a room that must deliver ultimate peace and comfort so a good night's rest is assured.

Yet despite its key role, the bedroom doesn't always get the planning attention or achieve the decorative status that it truly deserves. Precisely because it is located beyond the "public" zone, therefore unlikely to be seen by visitors, we may not consider it the ideal candidate for a new sofa or tailor-made storage. Busy people may see no point in creating a soothing room in which they sleep and get dressed during the twilight hours. But think about it in terms of quality of life: a night's stay in a boutique hotel bedroom may span less than twelve hours, but it can be uplifting and memorable. Don't we all deserve the equivalent every night of the year?

The bedroom's location is vital. First, consider the noise factor. In townhouses, the master bedroom is conventionally situated at the front of the house, but a smaller, garden-facing bedroom might be more tranquil if the house is on a busy road. If you are moving to a row house or apartment,

LEFT **The most tranquil bedrooms combine the spare lines of a modern hotel room with personal items that hold a special significance. Here all clutter is banished, while the contemporary furniture is tempered with pretty textiles, soothing colors, and a great view.**

remember to check out the noise coming from next door, in the morning and at night. It's impossible to counteract noisy neighbors, but you can at least avoid siting a bedroom adjacent to someone else's kitchen, with all its accompanying sound effects. If relocation of the bedroom is impossible, take practical measures. Consider double- or triple-glazing windows in a street-facing bedroom, or installing clothes storage, rather than the headboard, against a particularly noisy shared wall.

In a large house with many rooms, there's sometimes the luxury to pick the most secluded one for your bedroom. Good spots include a room at the end of a corridor, a bedroom leading off a small landing, or an attic eyrie. But if such physical separation isn't possible, minor structural alterations will help. Consider enclosing a staircase leading to all bedrooms and adding a door (at the top or base of the flight) to reduce

FAR LEFT **Although situated on a mezzanine, this bedroom is at the end of a corridor, so it retains a sense of seclusion.**

HERE **Simple decoration is the key to a tranquil bedroom: here, an all-white palette and built-in furniture impose Zenlike calm.**

RIGHT **In a new-built house, there is the luxury to site the bedroom close to lush greenery and views, guaranteeing peace.**

THIS PAGE AND FAR RIGHT, TOP **If the building has particularly dominant architectural features, use them as a decorative cue. In these two bedrooms, large plain windows overlook a garden and a lake respectively, so furniture and decoration has been kept simple** so as not to detract from the view. It's a matter of personal choice whether you screen the sunshine from a big picture window, or not. One owner has chosen to put in floor-to-ceiling blackout blinds, while the others (far right) have left windows unadorned.

FAR RIGHT, BOTTOM **The pretty period detailing in this country bedroom reflects a softer decorative approach. A white-on-white color scheme is interpreted with gathered curtains, and simple bed linen, to give a comfortable and romantic interior.**

noise and to mark the division between public and private zones. Or on a small landing, add a false partition wall a few feet before the bedroom entrance to create a small lobby accessed by a conventional door or sliding doors. If the bedroom itself is big, consider sectioning off the entry portion using floor-to-ceiling cabinets so that arrival into the bedroom proper is via a dressing area.

Once physical peace is assured, concentrate on mood. Defining and capturing one that makes you feel tranquil is the single most important factor to consider when planning a bedroom and must be done long before choosing colors or arranging furniture. To crystallize what works for you, scrutinize real bedrooms and spend time leafing through a pile of interiors magazines, tearing out pages that appeal. What is it about these rooms that makes them feel so good? Is it moody lighting or plain walls unadorned by pictures? Are you drawn to pale or dark colors? Think carefully: is there a bedroom, half-remembered, that once attracted you? What were its key elements? Even an imaginary bedroom, evocatively described in a book, can offer a starting point.

Whatever the chosen mood (romantic, uplifting), it must be translated into as simple a visual statement as possible. Purity of line, no extraneous furniture, and muted decoration (rather than clutter or pattern) is what makes most of us feel peaceful. Start the paring-back process from within. Emotionally, it's a false

Due to its size and function, the bed will dominate the bedroom, so pick a style that suits the chosen mood.

economy to build beautiful, seamless closets only for them to be overflowing and muddled inside. So before planning storage, have a major clearout. Give away clothes you no longer wear, banish suitcases to attic storage, and repatriate books to the sitting room. Be equally ruthless with existing bedroom furniture. The basics are a bed, beside tables, clothes storage, a mirror, and a chair. Find another home for everything else.

Due to its size and function, the bed will dominate the bedroom, so pick a style that suits the chosen mood. For those in search of monastic simplicity, a mattress or futon on a raised wooden or metal platform with unseen support looks particularly tranquil as it gives the impression of "floating" in mid-air. Alternatively, choose a plain divan skimming the floor on castors or metal legs, or a white-painted, utilitarian-looking metal bedframe. For the simplest of looks, avoid a headboard or, if you must have one, choose an unadorned rectangle of wood or upholstered plain fabric. A made-to-measure platform bed and headboard looks especially streamlined if designed to include a wall-mounted bedside shelf, thus doing away with the need for a bedside cabinet.

For a softer take on a simple bed, pick a plain style—such as an innocuous divan—that allows for a judicious and atmospheric ruffling of fabric. While pressed white bed linen, with hospital corners and Oxford border pillowcases, offers the right crisp simplicity on a platform bed, a divan looks inviting with floppy pillows and a lightly tossed bedcover. Provided textiles are kept plain and styling minimal, the look can be enhanced with drapes.

ABOVE LEFT **Focusing on monastic-style looks doesn't mean you must compromise on comfort. For the most inviting bed, pick goose-down pillows, a quality sprung mattress, and luxurious bedding, preferably with Egyptian cotton or linen sheets.**

ABOVE RIGHT **For those who value neatness, seamless storage is vital. This bedroom manages to stay uncluttered because all clothes and sports equipment are tucked into a walk-in closet beyond the sliding door.**

THIS PAGE **As ingenious as it is simple, this system of wall hooks makes for an instant clean-up, yet still looks chic. It works best combined with a closet and chest of drawers, however, as not every item of clothing will look as good as these distressed jeans.**

A ceiling-hung mosquito net is a classic and romantic choice, but consider also a plain wood or contemporary metal four-poster or an antique campaign-style bed hung with voile curtains. A wall-mounted carved or painted board corona draped with linen or wool looks pretty but restrained.

After the bed, storage is the next vital factor. A tranquil bedroom must have enough cupboards so that even the messiest person feels encouraged to clean up before going to sleep. After the initial cull of possessions, take time to assess what must be stored in the bedroom—clothes, toiletries, yoga mat, and so on—and how best these items may be arranged. While it's tempting to pick storage for its good looks, at least start off by confronting (honestly) your bedroom behavior. A messy person always in a rush will find wall hooks useful, while an organized individual may prefer everything stored in a floor-to-ceiling closet.

The successful tranquility of a bedroom depends on what is seen from the bed: it's not especially soothing, for example, to confront a

OPPOSITE PAGE, RIGHT **In a confined space, a freestanding armoire needs careful design to prevent it from overpowering the room. This one is successful because there's a generous gap between the top of the armoire and the ceiling.**

THIS PAGE **Spanning the central portion of the room, a block of cabinets forms a neat division between the master bedroom and the bathroom beyond.**

large pair of freestanding armoires on the opposite wall. In an ideal world, storage should be in an entirely separate room. Although we don't all have huge homes with lots of room to spare, there may be possibilities that you could consider. If there is a tiny spare bedroom next door to your bedroom that is rarely used, you could add an interconnecting door and plenty of built-ins to transform it into a dressing room. Alternatively, if an adjacent bedroom can't be spared in its entirety, steal a portion of it, adding a new plasterboard dividing wall to section off the new room and create a compact walk-in closet.

If there's no choice but to have armoires in the bedroom, there are plenty of ways to create elegant, "invisible" storage. Floor-to-ceiling flush doors, painted or fabric-covered to match the walls, are the most subtle option. Alternatively, mirrored doors or sand-blasted glass fronts can make a room seem bigger and look streamlined, though remember that the armoire's contents must be kept scrupulously neat behind translucent glass doors to avoid show-through. If bedroom walls are to be paneled, either with wood veneers or painted composite board, closet doors can be matched so there is a seamless link between the two.

However subtle the armoires look, positioning is still vital so that they don't overpower a small room. If there are fireplace cavities flanking a chimney breast, dressers will look neater built out to cover the entire wall, rather than squeezed into each alcove. Consider having a wall of cupboards across the bed-head wall, with fake flush panels behind the bed, so armoires can't be seen when you're lying down. In a big room, use cupboards as a space divider, perhaps with a connecting bathroom or dressing room behind. Design them to stop short of the ceiling with an access point at each end, so they divide, rather than dominate, the space.

Once closet space is sorted, plan the position of the bed so there are good things to see once lying down. The nicest option by far is to have a clear view through a window, if not of green fields, then at least of treetops. If you are planning the bedroom from scratch, perhaps in an attic re-model, then consider a floor-to-ceiling window or skylight that affords inspirational views. If there's no chance of a peaceful view, try to make sure the bed is at least facing a blank wall (which can feel peaceful in itself) or one hung with an inspiring picture. Weigh up the pros and cons of different bed positions. Most of us have an innate sense of what feels "right," but ask yourself some pertinent questions. If the room is east-facing (and you are a light sleeper), will it be annoying to be awoken with a sharp burst of sunshine? If you like to sleep with the door open at night, will having the head of the bed close to the door feel wrong?

OPPOSITE PAGE, LEFT **Plan a variety of storage solutions to suit your needs. While clothes are best out of sight, books, music, or great accessories—such as shoes—can be used as a decorative focus. Here, floor-to-ceiling bookshelves add personality, as well as inspiring a color scheme.**

OPPOSITE PAGE, RIGHT **In a compact bedroom, with scant space for built-in storage, a freestanding cabinet makes a good choice. Look for an unusual piece that's practical as well as attractive.**

THIS PAGE **An all-white scheme may need a hint of accent color to add zest. In this room, the overlapping white tones are highlighted with the gilded dressing table and a glint of turquoise glass.**

Color dramatically affects the mood of a room, but address it only after space planning. Think of it as an overall statement—encompassing walls, flooring, curtains, and bedding—rather than choose a paint color, or bed cover, in isolation. Aim for a bedroom suffused with just one shade, or several gently overlapping tones, rather than for a cleverly decorated room with well-defined areas of color. That way, the boundaries between horizontal and vertical planes become blurred, and the overall mood is calmer. It's fun to add the odd contrasting throw or piece of furniture, but try to keep the fundamentals working together to create a soothing whole.

White on white is, of course, an obvious choice and has endless variations. Used in combination with very simple, monastic-style furniture, it will certainly look pure, but can also be stark. To make white seem fresh, yet still welcoming, there are plenty of tricks to employ. Scan the white options on a paint chart and pick warmer versions of pure brilliant white, adding in gentle gray tones or a creamy shade. Consider painting two

walls white and two off-white, or use several complementary shades to pick out molding or paintwork. Pay attention to textures: white paired with sand-blasted glass closet doors can look clinical, but combined with linen curtains, fluffy blankets, and gloss woodwork, it will develop a sensual, uplifting mood.

For those who find deeper colors more soothing, walls can be painted in a variety of subtle neutrals, from biscuit to gray-blue, or covered with a plain, textural fabric such as felt or linen. Always keep walls plain in the bedroom, as patterned wallpaper can look startling first thing in the morning. Classic white woodwork also makes too much of a contrast against soft, moody shades. Instead, pick a much paler tone of the wall color for baseboards, doors, and window frames. Don't overlook wood veneer paneling as a soothing surface. A rich tone and a good grain look beautiful and, particularly if used on walls and floor, will give the room a womblike feel. A wall of books can have a similar effect.

Window treatments must be selected to control light flow. On weekends and vacations, it can be wonderful to be woken early by the sun, but we all need to sleep in sometimes or rest during the day if feeling unwell. So make sure that there are adequate ways to create a darkened room. Interlined curtains, a plain shade teamed with unlined curtains, or slatted wooden Venetian blinds are particularly effective. Think, too, about privacy: if the bedroom is visible from outside, you won't want to have to close the curtains every time you want to get changed in order to remain unseen. A translucent Roman shade or voile or net, flat unlined cotton "panels" or replacing clear windowpanes with sand-blasted glass are all attractive options. Even better, they will all filter sunlight prettily, promoting a soothing ambience.

Lighting matters. Don't dispense with good overhead illumination: in winter many of us need to get dressed in the morning while it's still dark outside. Try combining overhead lighting with wall lamps for mid-level

OPPOSITE PAGE, LEFT **If you find moody colors soothing, but dark walls overpowering, introduce deep tones seasonally, focusing on the bed. This gray cover looks welcoming in winter, but can be removed for a clean, all-white summer look.**

OPPOSITE PAGE, RIGHT **Overlapping middle tones look peaceful and are a space-enhancing choice in a small room with a low ceiling. Accessorize with contrasting dark wood and pure white bedding for a sophisticated finish.**

ABOVE LEFT **For some, the appeal of the all-white bedroom is that the walls provide a blank canvas for personal paintings, drawings, and photographs. Keep the look restrained by choosing images according to a particular theme.**

ABOVE RIGHT **To keep a one-color scheme from appearing visually bland, concentrate on tiny decorative details. At a distance, this cutwork pillowcase and glass-beaded lamp blend into one simple, pure interior: close-up, they add depth and interest.**

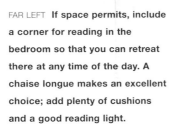

FAR LEFT **If space permits, include a corner for reading in the bedroom so that you can retreat there at any time of the day. A chaise longue makes an excellent choice; add plenty of cushions and a good reading light.**

HERE **Bedroom seating must look and feel inviting, so steer clear of metal or plastic utility-style chairs. Instead pick upholstered carver chairs or a low-level ottoman, beanbags, or seating cubes.**

RIGHT **However tiny the bedroom, try to include at least one chair. It's the ultimate multifunctional piece, providing a spot for hanging clothes, a perch for contemplation, and somewhere to lounge post-bath, pre-bed.**

illumination. Bedside lighting must be efficient for reading, yet discreet. It's a good idea to install wall-mounted lights on each side of the bed or directly above it so the bedside table is kept free of extraneous clutter. If there is a seating area in the bedroom, you may need to include a floor lamp, more wall-mounted lights, or a gooseneck lamp, too. Always add a dimmer switch to bedroom lighting and position light switches by the bed as well as by the door so you can control the atmosphere, hotel-style, while lying down.

If there is space, try to include some seating in the bedroom. Even a plain dining chair placed beneath a window can provide a quiet spot to gather your thoughts. Better still, an upholstered stool at the foot of the bed, a cozy armchair, or a scaled-down sofa will transform a bedroom from merely a place to sleep to a sanctuary for relaxing, even providing a perch for visiting partners or children. A dressing table or writing desk (but not a computer desk) is the ultimate bedroom extra. If there's abundant space, group several small armchairs or ottomans around a tiny table for relaxed breakfasts. Decide whether a TV will be a source of irritation or provide an excuse for relaxing in bed. If space is tight, you could position one on an extendable arm.

Remember that a soothing bedroom is also a personal retreat. Some individuals thrive on a room stripped bare, but the majority of us like to have special possessions around us: a favorite painting, perhaps, a precious piece of furniture, or some treasured family photographs. So indulge yourself. Add in the things that you really enjoy and would prefer to keep private from visitors downstairs. Take time to make the bedroom a comfortable, tranquil place, and you will find yourself withdrawing there long before the official close of day.

Take time to create a bathroom that is truly peaceful—a room in which washing is enjoyable is worth twenty trips to the spa.

A room that must be planned and constructed with maximum practicality in mind, the bathroom also possesses the greatest potential to soothe. This should come as no surprise: everyone responds positively to the sound of running water and to the splash of it on bare skin, both in the natural world and in the washroom. Increasingly, spas, Turkish baths, and saunas are becoming popular places in which to unwind outside the home, and these days we naturally associate the bathroom with relaxing. A bathroom also promises to be a private place, where we shut the door on the world to be alone.

That's the theory, and in recent years an increasing number of bathrooms and shower rooms have been included in our homes. If space permits, it's considered de rigueur to have a connecting bathroom off the master bedroom, if not one in every guest room. The bathroom now vies with the kitchen as a status symbol, with architects and interior designers churning out state-of-the-art designs. Yet it's debatable whether such expensively outfitted rooms—efficient as they are—actively promote relaxation. So take time to create a bathroom that is truly peaceful—a room in which washing is as enjoyable as twenty trips to the spa.

Early on, define a mood and look that soothes you. Sporty, active individuals will relish a pristine, sparkling washroom, reminiscent of showers at the gym. Others may want a chill-out zone, a

RIGHT **A good bathroom should make you feel energized first thing in the morning, yet should also be a relaxing place to be at the end of the day. This one combines both qualities, with its crisp towels and shaving mirror for morning and neat stool for evening preparation.**

soothing
bathrooms

Look closely at your bathtime rituals. Do you prefer to splash and dash or linger in the bath?

THIS PAGE **If you're creating a new bathroom, remember that good space planning makes all the difference to a feeling of serenity. By placing this tub centrally, beneath the skylight, the owner has allowed plenty of room to circulate, as well as for a comfortable armchair.**

OPPOSITE PAGE **Two small interconnecting rooms offer a good alternative to a single large family bathroom for adults in search of bathtime peace. Here, the bathtub is in one room, the sink and shower in the other.**

bathroom with a peaceful picture window onto a garden, or space for a terrycloth-covered armchair. For some, it will be the back-to-nature simplicity of a stone-walled, wet-room shower that appeals. Everything you pick—from bath fixtures to surfaces—should be geared to achieving that ambience.

First, consider the facilities already at your disposal. What must stay and what can be changed? A family bathroom will need to combine practicality with simplicity, whereas an existing connecting bathroom may be more tailored to your needs. The number of people using the bathroom dictates how self-indulgent the design is (or how great a financial investment you're prepared to make). If it's possible to design a bathroom from scratch as a result of adding an attic extension or creating a new-built house, this is the ideal opportunity to include special extras, such as computerized lighting and music.

Size needn't be an issue. Of course, it's luxurious to convert a bedroom into a new bathroom with a central bathtub. But even the tiniest bathroom, cleverly conceived, can feel calm. Draw up a to-scale floor plan, with cut-out shapes of bath fixtures, and spend time figuring out the best layout. Replacing a pedestal sink with a wall-mounted one or devising a custom-built combined tub/shower design can make all the difference. Decide now on whether you want a bathtub or a shower, or both. Most of us have a natural preference. What's yours, what's your partner's? Look closely at your bathtime rituals. Do you prefer to splash and dash or linger in the bath? If you are a shower person, it might be best to dispense with a bathtub altogether and invest in a full-size shower or a wet-room instead.

Efficient plumbing and heating are very important. A bathroom must not only look

soothing, but must also be comfortable to be in (naked or clothed). If the room is chilly, add underfloor heating, and consider a heated towel rod (in a tiny space, this may be combined with a wall-mounted radiator). If the water pressure is frustratingly weak, install a pump. Talking to a good plumber early on is essential: he will be able to translate your needs into practicalities and will save you money in the long term. (If you balk at the cost of good plumbing, remember that the bathroom is used at least twice daily, so it's always worth the investment to get it right.)

A good bathtub should be comfortable enough to relax in and attractive to look at. For those who love to soak, a straight-sided style with plenty of depth is ideal. Long is also good, but match the dimensions to your height. If your feet won't reach the end of the tub, it will be awkward

to lie in comfortably. With its sloping end, a roll-top bathtub is a classic, lounge-worthy choice. An oval version is similarly ergonomic. Think about materials: acrylic may be warm, but it's squeaky; traditional heavy-gauge steel, by contrast, retains the water's heat. For the adventurous, there are cozy options like a hardwood Japanese-style bathtub; a stainless steel or stone one, on the other hand, looks good but lacks comfort.

Think, too, about luxurious extras. These days, it's no longer considered a cliché to install a whirlpool in the bathtub. There are very sophisticated options, so it's worth investigating choices at a specialized designer bath store. Whirlpool or hydro-massage systems—with the option of back and foot massage jets—can be installed into many conventional bathtub styles.

OPPOSITE PAGE, LEFT **A roll-top tub is comfortable, but if your look is chic modern, rather than period, conceal the traditional legs within a wooden box or replace them with a concrete block, as here.**

OPPOSITE PAGE, RIGHT **We can't all enjoy an inspiring picture-window view like this one from a bath, but try to allow for some natural daylight, perhaps by placing the bathtub beneath a skylight.**

LEFT **Provide additional privacy by surrounding the tub with floor-to-ceiling curtains. For a pretty option, layer a white waterproof curtain with linen, cotton, or lace drapes on the outside.**

BELOW **For the ultimate serene bathing experience, choose a simple, yet beautiful tub, with minimalist faucets, and tuck it into a quiet corner. Towels, lotions, and accessories can be wheeled in, when necessary, on a trolley.**

OPPOSITE PAGE **For some, a relaxed bathroom is also a sociable one. This luxurious space has twin heads in the shower enclosure, as well as a large bathtub, to cater to all.**

FAR LEFT AND BELOW LEFT **In a small bathroom, a shower enclosure without a door feels less claustrophobic and—critically— requires less space. Curved walls offer a particularly intimate look, while a floor-to-ceiling dividing wall affords privacy between the shower area and the toilet.**

LEFT **A good shower should make you feel uplifted, as well as being functional. Here, a gecko door handle and moody concrete walls create a dramatic effect.**

If possible, wall-mount faucets, which gives a cleaner silhouette. Centrally situated faucets are great if you regularly bathe à *deux*, so no one gets the faucet end. If a rectangular tub is to be inset into a tiled or glass-topped surround, make sure it is deep enough to hold toiletries or a cup of tea. A roll-top tub will require a nearby chair or a wall-mounted shelf. Make sure a towel rod is within grab-distance of the bathtub, and—if possible—that there's a pleasing view from the bath-level eye-line.

For the most relaxing shower, address the size of enclosure first—the bigger, the better, so there's plenty of elbow room. Self-contained shower enclosures are available in increasingly large sizes, often with a built-in seat or dual shower areas. A conventional square shower tray can be extended with a tiled surface on one side and a standard glass door inset into narrow walls. The best option of all is to design a custom-made shower, sectioning it off with a curved partition wall or enclosing it in a dramatic all-glass box, to suit the available space. In tiny bathrooms, substitute a stationary sand-blasted panel for a conventional hinged shower door.

Invest as much as possible in a good showerhead (as well as a pump if water pressure is low). For a waterfall-style deluge, pick a large, classic-style, ceiling-mounted shower rose, preferably with different spray modes. A power-shower, by contrast, is energizing, so choose one with a selection of massage sprays and jets. Contemporary shower enclosures may also include a steam sauna, mood-evoking colored lights, and aromatherapy-dispensing mechanisms. Think about comfort underfoot: in addition to the classic ceramic tray, there are now myriad options, including inset stone slabs, circular stainless steel, and slatted teak trays.

If space permits, a wet-room shower, preferably with a toilet and wall-mounted sink, offers the ultimate in relaxation. Seek professional advice from a builder or architect on waterproofing and to check if the floor is load-bearing—particularly crucial if you want to line the shower with stone slabs. Wet-room showers look best when walls and floors blend into a seamless whole, so choose stone or tiles that offer adequate grip underfoot: mosaics, limestone, and slate are all good options. If the wet-room is on the top floor, consider a skylight, or, if it faces onto a private yard, think about a sliver of floor-to-ceiling window to let in sunlight.

Sink choice depends on the look you're after and the way you want to use the bathroom. In a pure, minimalist space, a wall-mounted stainless-steel or stone rectangular sink might be the best solution, but if you want to create a classic look, a white ceramic, rectangular pedestal is a practical yet luxurious choice. Whatever style you opt for, pick a basin that is wide, so water won't splash out easily, with a ledge deep enough to rest toiletries and shaving equipment on; one that has a built-in towel rod is particularly useful.

If the bath or shower room is to double as a dressing room, a vanity-style unit is a good idea. An arrangement of a bowl-style basin on a counter or sinks inset into a stone top looks streamlined, provides plenty of room for toiletries, and—provided the counter is at a suitable height—the addition of a stool turns it into a dressing table. Look for a freestanding vanity unit with shelves beneath or plan a built-in area to include drawers. Less attractive necessities can be stored out of view with only the prettiest jars on show. A well-illuminated mirror (consider an anti-mist mechanism) and wall-mounted magnifying/shaving mirror are useful.

Given the amount of time we spend undressed in the bathroom, it's vital to pick feel-good textures. You need to weigh the benefit of choosing traditionally non-bathroom materials, such as wallpaper, fabrics, or carpet, which look and feel comforting, versus the importance of practical, water-

RIGHT **In a tiny city bathroom, it's vital to keep the sink area clutter free. The sleek glass counter has been designed with vanity units below, providing ample storage.**

FAR RIGHT **This bathroom is adjacent to a dressing room and has been designed with simple elegance in mind. A washstand teamed with a dramatic wall-hung mirror looks decorative and provides a visual link between the bathroom and dressing room.**

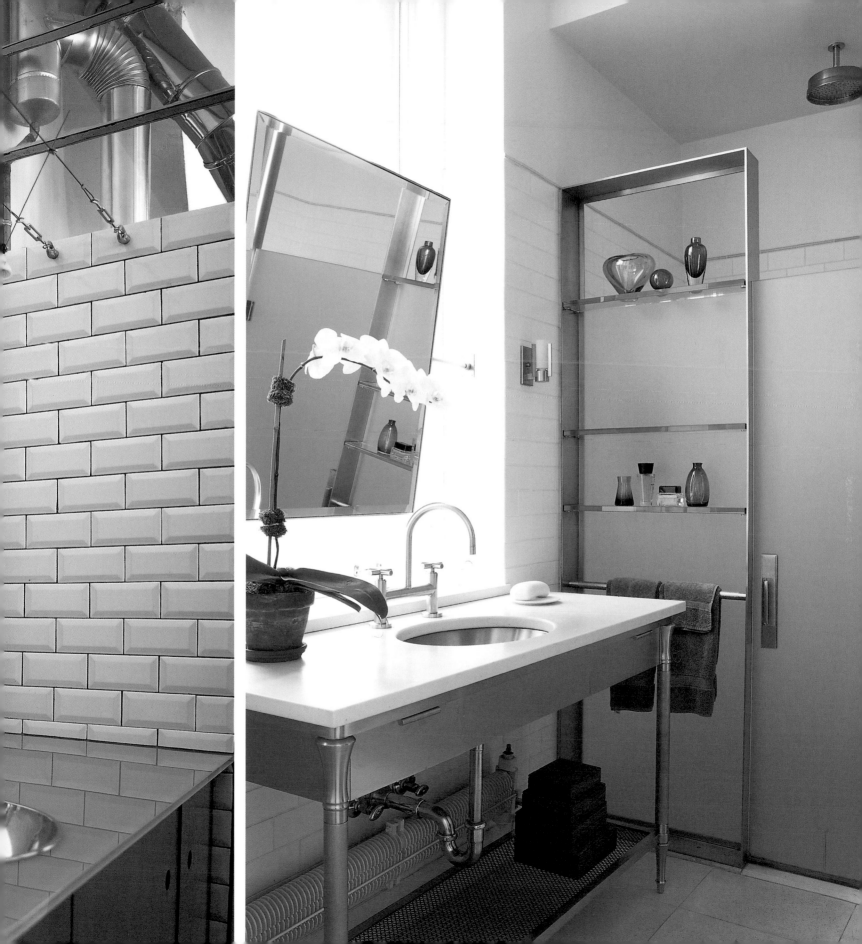

resistant surfaces like ceramic tiles or stone. Before choosing, re-examine the mood you seek to achieve: is it energizing, peaceful, or pure? The surfaces you pick will directly affect ambience and—precisely because they cover all key areas in the bathroom—will dominate the color scheme.

Natural materials like stone and wood are often expensive, but can be worth the investment. They come in neutral, gently variegated colors and patterns, so they are easy on the eye. Stone, including limestone, marble, granite, and slate, is waterproof (though it must be properly sealed) so it is perfect for everything from floors to shower enclosures. Solid wood is also water-resistant, especially hardwoods such as teak and iroko, but steer clear of veneers, which may "lift" if damaged by water. In addition to making practical countertops, both stone and wood can be carved into sinks, shower trays, and even bathtubs that feel natural.

Tiles, by contrast, provide an energizing, uplifting mood. Take them from floor to ceiling, rather than restricting them to a shower or bathtub enclosure, to create a glistening vertical plane of color and texture. In a pure, simple bathroom, choose plain, oblong metro-style or square tiles, or, for a more sophisticated look, pick glass mosaics, metal-finish tiles, or color-glazed ceramics. If you are planning to use matching tiles on the floor and walls, make sure the texture and thickness are suitable for use underfoot. Tiles are also the best medium for introducing color in a bathroom. Choose white for ultimate calm, or use ocean colors, from dark turquoise to sea-green or the palest eau de nil.

If tiles feel clinical, consider surfaces that can be used in unbroken lengths for a seam-free finish. Stainless steel and sand-blasted glass look pure and simple, or consider neutral-colored

Before choosing surfaces for a bathroom, re-examine the mood you seek to achieve: is it energizing, peaceful, or pure?

OPPOSITE PAGE **Mosaic tiles offer a practical, yet beautiful, option for wet-rooms and showers. With their unrivaled intensity of color, they have the ability to transform the most humble space into a custom-made washroom.**

THIS PAGE **For a pared-down bathroom with a quietly luxurious mood, choose slabs of stone in pale, soothing colors. Floor-to-ceiling stone can appear bland, so contrast it with a mirror, sand-blasted glass, or steel.**

laminate wall panels, Corian for counters and floors, or poured concrete. If you prefer matte, warm surfaces, then flooring options include rubber tiles, linoleum, and sealed cork. Ordinary floorboards, sanded and waxed or painted with gloss floor paint, are inexpensive and feel comforting underfoot. Walls may be painted or think about a textural wall finish: polished plaster or a muted paint effect, sealed with a glaze, adds gentle pattern, yet is water resistant.

We assume the bathroom to be a private retreat, but in a busy household, that's not always possible. A lock helps, of course, but we don't all want to bathe behind closed doors. Take simple measures to protect modesty. Plan the bathroom layout so passersby on the stairs don't stare straight into the shower or at the toilet. Consider partitioning off the toilet, tucking it behind a floor-to-ceiling partition wall or housing it within a simple cubicle. A freestanding bathtub may be prettily screened with a shower curtain on a ceiling-mounted rod or fitted into a natural alcove with a sand-blasted glass screen. Protecting privacy in the shower is particularly easy with a tiled partition wall, glass-brick wall, or a curved, acid-etched, freestanding enclosure.

Windows also require screening, but remember that the prime purpose is to prevent someone from seeing in rather than to provide darkness conducive to sleep. Sheer, light-diffusing window treatments are the answer, and blinds make the most practical and good-looking choice. Many modern styles come in useful variants, from bottom-up styles, which screen the lower half of the window only, to half-fabric, half-mesh versions, which still let in light. Plantation shutters and Venetian blinds filter light prettily, while sheer voile or linen Roman shades add softness to counteract the hard surfaces. Alternatively, consider replacing clear glass windowpanes with acid-etched panels.

Well-planned lighting and sound are vital for ambience. Of course, you will want good overhead illumination, but tailor additional lighting to your needs. Flank the bathroom mirror with discreet wall lights for good make-up illumination or add an angled spotlight close to a shaving mirror. And don't overlook the power of candlelight to create a peaceful atmosphere for bathing. If music is important to you, it's comparatively easy (and inexpensive) to install ceiling speakers in the bathroom with central controls located elsewhere in the house. If you're on a low budget, a transistor radio does just as well. Think about including wave sound effects or birdsong among more conventional music CDs. These days, it is even possible to wall-mount a specialist waterproof LCD TV isolated from mains power in the bathroom, though you will need to make sure it is installed by a specialized audio-visual company.

FAR LEFT, TOP **Every bathroom, however plain and serene, needs its little luxuries to promote relaxation, whether fluffy towels, candles, or perfumed bath oils. Gather them onto a tabletop, or store in a cabinet on wheels.**

FAR LEFT, BOTTOM **We all have different criteria for relaxing. If a TV in the bathroom seems like heaven, but is too costly, then consider a compromise. It may be worth opting for less expensive bathroom fixtures and investing in a good entertainment system.**

LEFT **There's an appealing intimacy about curtains around the bathtub, allowing you to talk with a friend and still preserve modesty. Site faucets centrally so the curtains will drape attractively over either end of the tub.**

ABOVE **Most bathrooms are visible to outsiders, so it's vital to cover windows with simple but attractive screens. Match window treatments to the prevailing style: pure white cotton shades are a perfect choice for this crisp, luxurious bathroom.**

quiet corners

We all need time out from life's pressures, for reflection, forward planning, or thoughtful conversation with selected individuals. In an office environment, privacy is assured by closing a door or sliding screens shut. In the wider world, we'll seek an intimate restaurant for our peaceful moments, or a boutique hotel for a night away. But at home—where, sometimes, time out matters most—we may forget to engineer quiet corners and ambience-inducing areas among the principal rooms.

So take time to redress that balance. Most homes will have the occasional "spare" or "dead" space that can be transformed into a usable, proactive area, from a compact hall or turn in the corridor to an attic floor ripe for conversion. These quiet zones occupy minimal room, but allow for physical (and mental) breathing space.

For those of us choosing to live in modern, open-plan environments, finding a quiet spot isn't so much about stealing square inches as about dividing up the available space to create privacy. Whether you choose opaque or translucent partitions, sliding or fixed, horizontal or vertical, will depend as much on your personal vision of privacy as on the style you wish to create at home. But the successful balance will be a mix of sociable, wide-open spaces and the intimate zones that we naturally crave.

Halls, landings, and corridors are rich in space potential and useful to exploit because they fall silent and empty for much of the day.

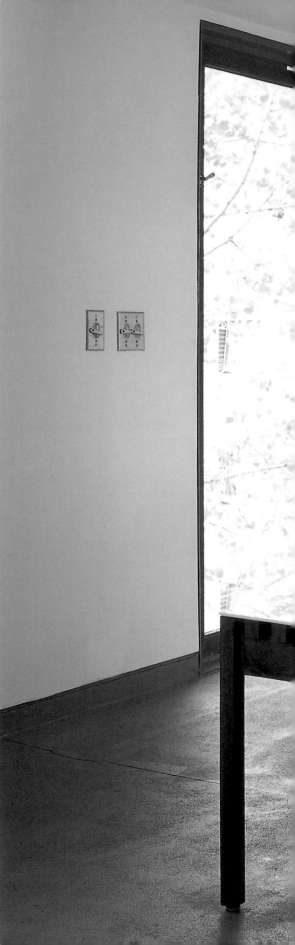

Every home, however tiny, has its odd spaces. Frequently overlooked spots include natural stopping points, such as a landing or the end of a corridor, and architectural features, such as wall recesses or a vestibule. These are the areas bypassed on the way to principal rooms, more likely to be ignored than celebrated. It's worth assessing these "spare" corners: with clever planning, they provide pint-sized retreats and, in a small home, make precious square feet work even harder. If there's no room for a study, for example, you might try tucking a desk onto a landing.

Transforming a corner might mean the simple addition of a chair: in today's busy world, it's appealing to create a dedicated perch for contemplation. A solitary stool becomes the beatific (and grown-up) antithesis of a child's "naughty" chair, a place to silently chant a mantra or somewhere to collect your thoughts. You might even dedicate one chair, in assorted spots, to each member of the family. Pick furniture that offers good sitting support, but that is slim enough not to impede passers-by on a narrow walkway. Seating in a corridor is quite plainly not for lounging on, so a high-backed chair, stool with footrests, or salon-style armchair is ideal—but consciously avoid dumping bags here!

It's important to decorate the area so that the corner looks enticing on approach, provides an uplifting view once you're seated, and adds a decorative focus to a larger space. Visually, a chair is always a clever way to add interest in a corridor. Color, texture, and pattern are all useful tools.

PREVIOUS PAGE **Choose a dramatic-looking chair, in wild upholstery or with a pretty silhouette, to make a decorative statement in an entrance hall or on a landing. Place it in a natural pool of sunlight for added emphasis.**

RIGHT **In an open-plan space such as this, a chair and table create a visual and practical link between the narrow entrance corridor and the main room beyond. If space seems tight, work out where to place furniture on a floor plan.**

corners &
corridors

LEFT **Carefully assess traffic areas, then think laterally about how to make the best use of the existing space. In this modern, double-height home, the owner has utilized spare ceiling space, rather than the hall floor area, to create a quiet corner for reading—as well as an occasional spare bed.**

RIGHT **A tiny upstairs landing—too narrow for a major piece of furniture—is transformed into a contemplative perch with the addition of a stool. Have fun with color, picking out strong shades to stimulate, or moody subtle ones to calm things down.**

FAR RIGHT **In a small hallway or a turn in the corridor, consider adding a chair and a telephone, so that you can carry out conversations in private and comfort. Add storage for telephone books, paper, and pens, with a low enough surface for making notes.**

Consider painting the section of wall behind a chair in a saturated shade from cherry red to leafy green, wallpaper a small landing in a large-scale design, or treat an alcove to a textural finish. Against white walls, vibrant upholstery stands out well. It's ideal if the chair is close to the window so that you can enjoy a good view. But if not, hang a large mirror on an adjacent wall to capture reflected treetops or to bounce back a twist of corridor. Or, wall-mount a collection of photographs directly opposite. If you want a spot where you can just sit and think, avoid adding bookshelves or a telephone.

Halls, landings, and corridors are rich in space potential and useful to exploit because, though busy at key times, they fall silent and empty for much of the day. Most of us struggle with tiny entrances, but don't give up. Measure the floor area, draw a scale plan, and think laterally. One wall of a corridor may be lined with bookshelves and, with an added chair, becomes a library. A compact entrance hall may be turned into a study, with a built-in counter and recessed shelves on one side, or a generously sized landing enclosed with floor-to-ceiling glass doors to create a semi-private reading room. Such additions give the illusion of more, not less, space.

In setting up a quiet corner in a "public" hall or corridor, remember that some activities are better suited to the space than others. A desk area, a corner for phone calls, or an armchair for doing the crossword are all ideal, whereas messy pursuits that involve gear, such as sewing or art, should be relegated to a workroom. Do make comfort a priority because halls can be drafty and chilly. Consider underfloor heating or an extra radiator to boost heat, or add a freestanding screen around the quiet zone. In a modern property, a glass booth for phone calls can be an amusing, dramatic option.

Precisely because halls and landings are often gloomy, it's crucial to employ tricks to bring in light. Otherwise, they will never become uplifting places to sit. Consider inserting a skylight to flood

RIGHT **Odd corners deserve the same decorative attention as the main rooms in the house, but because they are viewed in isolation, you can afford to include more frivolous detailing.**

FAR RIGHT, TOP **Creating a natural sense of separation from the kitchen itself, this bay window forms the perfect eating area. The decorative light and cushions enhance the transition between cooking and entertainment zones.**

FAR RIGHT, BOTTOM **Not all windowseats need be solitary. This one—part of an open-plan kitchen—offers a slim perch within a larger activity space.**

sunshine onto a top-floor landing. In addition to conventional Velux windows, you can choose from polycarbonate ceiling domes, which come in circular, pyramid, or square designs, or an arched conservatory-style skylight. On a ground floor, adding internal windows in walls, or glass panels above internal doors, also assists light flow. A more radical (though expensive) option is to substitute acid-etched glass door panels for the traditional wooden ones, or—in a modern property—replace the doors with frameless laminated-glass ones.

In older properties, recessed windows provide a natural and more structured spot for a quiet corner. Thick walls flanking a window are perfect for filling in with a windowseat. Make it practical, as well as a thing of beauty, by including a lift-up storage seat, and match the style of carpentry to prevailing architectural features. Even if you're building a modern extension, it's a good idea to include a windowseat beneath a main window or to add a glassed-in nook on a mezzanine floor. The seat's dimensions should be tailored to allow for a comfortable depth, even if it isn't long enough to fully stretch out your legs on. A windowseat is a good way to enliven a side window, which may have a boring view. Add sand-blasted glass panes and a smartly upholstered cushion to distract the eye.

A bay window may also be fitted with a windowseat, but, even better, it provides space for a freestanding piece of furniture, such as a desk or daybed. Yet a bay needs careful planning if the arrangement is to look elegant: a sofa that is too large, for example, will overpower the niche. So make sure the height of furniture doesn't rise above the base of the windows; otherwise, the architectural balance (and view) will be destroyed. It's a good idea to tailor a bay window space to a specific activity. In a kitchen, it could contain a tiny table and stools to create an intimate eating zone or a space to read the papers. In a bedroom, a slim desk tucked beneath the window provides room for daily catch-up on paperwork.

LEFT AND BELOW **In a period property where several small rooms have been knocked together to create an open-plan space, spare "linking" areas may result. In this house, a wide corridor leading to bedroom and bathroom has been furnished with a comfortable sofa, creating an extra relaxing zone. Cleverly, one set of windows has been retained to offer leafy views while the others have been sand-blasted. The resulting play of light in the room is in turns soothing and dramatic.**

Open staircases
need furniture with
a good silhouette,
as a flight of stairs
naturally frames
what sits below
or beside it.

Windowseats enjoy ample daylight, but add mesh blinds or slatted shutters to control direct sunshine and to ensure privacy if the seat is street-facing. Instead of hanging curtains within the recess, which may look clumsy, hang thick, interlined drapes that will conceal the windowseat entirely when closed—fun for a private read. Plan artificial lighting to fit into the niche. Freestanding lamps are easily knocked over; instead, inset low-voltage downlights above the recess, add a wall-mounted spotlight, or fix an adjustable pendant light, which can be brought low for an intimate atmosphere.

Check out the hall for useful alcoves or cavities to exploit. The understairs area is an obvious choice, but too often we turn it into a broom cupboard or a powder room. The style of staircase—and the hall—will dictate, in part, how you use the space. A boxed-in staircase will look best fitted with a built-in desk and shelves, but if the staircase is part of an open-plan sitting area, incorporating a banquette or a bookcase might be a good idea. Make the area easy to clear up by adding drawers, cupboards, or storage boxes. Remember that the hall is a public place: you don't want casual visitors checking out your credit card bills. Open staircases, by contrast, need furniture with a good silhouette, as a flight of stairs naturally frames what sits below it—or beside it, in the case of a spiral. For a modern, cantilevered staircase, which by its very nature appears to "float" off the wall, pick furniture in light-diffusing materials—a glass-topped trestle table or an acrylic chair, perhaps. In a traditional property, with a weathered-wood staircase, an antique writing desk teamed with an upholstered dining chair would be infinitely more appropriate.

OPPOSITE PAGE **If a large entertaining area has a natural alcove or "dead" space between dominant architectural features, then exploit the space. Such naturally secluded spots lend themselves to the addition of a small cozy sofa, desk, or even a card table.**

ABOVE LEFT **Some landings may be generous enough in size to be furnished with an intimate grouping of armchairs. You can enhance the cozy mood by choosing furniture with curved silhouettes and tactile upholstery and adding plenty of cushions.**

ABOVE RIGHT **This ingenious nook, tucked below a staircase, has been cleverly furnished to make it appear bigger than it really is. The comfortable cushions and horizontal stripes add width, while the low-slung floor lamp focuses the eye firmly onto the bench.**

It's vital to designate a zone that can offer a retreat without necessarily being hidden away behind closed doors.

During the last decade, many of us have embraced open-plan living at home. Yet for all the light, space, and sociability that it brings, it can also be a double-edged sword. In a single, large, multifunctional room, with assorted family members and visitors all doing their own thing, it can be very tricky to find a noise-free space or an intimate area to share with friends. And in a converted attic or open-plan loft, with all living and eating spaces interconnected and no separate sitting room, it's even more important to create a cozy nook. It's human nature to want to hunker down in a small corner to relax, yet the typical open-plan area doesn't supply such spaces. So it's vital to designate a zone in the planning stage that can offer a retreat without necessarily being hidden away behind closed doors.

If you require total privacy or acoustic control, physical partitions or a mezzanine level will be the only answer. But subtle details like furniture arrangement, careful lighting, and contrasting materials go a long way to creating powerful, yet invisible, dividing lines between zones. First focus on why you need a quiet area, and who needs it? Is there someone who likes to read while others watch TV? Is it vital to have an intimate dining area for grown-ups in addition to the family kitchen table? Tailor your plans accordingly. Concentrate on playing up the open spaces designed for entertaining/activity—the "public" areas—and hone a cozy mood in the quiet ones.

RIGHT **It's important to lavish as much care and attention on a small, quiet eating zone as you might give to a more formal dining room. This one, which is tucked at the far end of an open-plan kitchen, enjoys leafy garden views and is furnished with chic, modern furniture.**

secluded
spots

An easy structural way to delineate space is to play with horizontal levels. The ceilings in industrial conversions can be unnaturally high, making noise echo and the space seem unfriendly. So to give character to a large room, as well as to mark out a more intimate section, consider dropping the ceiling in one place, perhaps over a dining table or in the TV zone. Think, too, of altering floor levels. The act of stepping up, or down, into a separate area is the open-plan equivalent of opening a door. If you are contemplating radical construction work, consider creating a sunken conversation pit that can be filled with cushions.

The arrangement of furniture is a simple way of creating a vital division between public areas that visitors can use and private, quiet spots. In a typical open-plan living space with no physical walls and boasting a kitchen, an island unit, table and chairs, and a sitting area, visitors will, unsurprisingly, feel free to congregate anywhere. But a tall bookcase, freestanding screen, or sofas placed back to

back will impose a convincingly solid division. A low daybed or a console table works similarly well and is effective in a smaller space because it won't impede the view from one end of the room to the other. For a more subtle division, experiment with furniture "body language." A solitary chair deliberately angled away from the "public" zone and accessorized with a floor lamp, for example, is quite clearly intended for private use, and visitors will keep well away.

Even for the family, it's worth making a distinction between the main sitting area and a quieter spot. This can be engineered with clever furniture arrangement and careful style choices. The key to a sociable open-plan relaxation zone is to choose a flexible combination of seating, such as large-scale sofas or modular pieces, arranged in a U- or L-shaped configuration. The area must be easy to get to from other activity zones and within communicating distance of the kitchen/eating zones.

OPPOSITE PAGE, LEFT AND RIGHT
A secluded zone needs to feel cozy for those sitting in it, yet look good as a part of the entire open-plan area. In this urban loft, the key has been to choose furniture with neat, low-slung silhouettes so that the grouping doesn't overpower the entire space. Cool white tones, combined with small bursts of color provided by a collection of turquoise glass on the window-sill, achieves an inviting and tranquil balance.

ABOVE LEFT **This pretty open-plan area combines free-standing furniture with a dropped ceiling to subtly divide sitting and eating spaces. The room looks cohesive because the decoration throughout is neutral in tone.**

ABOVE RIGHT **In a smaller open-plan space, it's not physical separation but subtle decorative changes that mark out a quiet spot. Here, the workmanlike chair and task lighting subtly separate a work zone from the relaxation area.**

By contrast, the creation of a secluded sitting area requires different criteria. For a start, you will need fewer pieces: just a chair or two, or a two-seater sofa and low table, can be enough. Upholstery pieces should be small and neat in outline to promote an intimate, enclosed mood. It's worth investigating various options in a good furniture store: think about high-backed armchairs, egg-shaped ceiling-suspension chairs, or a more formal three-seater bench style with molded individual seats, for example. Furniture should be arranged in a tight group, preferably facing toward a window and away from the main body of the room, so that a sense of division is clear to all. If there's not enough space for large pieces here, an attractive table and chairs can be an excellent alternative.

For some of us, it's more important to create an intimate eating zone that is separate from the open-plan heart of the kitchen. Just by moving the table and chairs a few feet away, perhaps tucking them beneath a window or behind a screen, you can make an appreciable difference to mood. Furniture choices will be key to making this intimate spot work well. Round tables are preferable to square ones because they fit into tighter spaces and feel more sociable. A pedestal style is particularly cozy, while a curved breakfast bar makes a good alternative in a small space. Visually, two chairs pulled up to a table look more inviting than a circle of seating. So choose fold-up or stacking styles, only bringing out extras when they are needed. Built-in bench seating around a small table also looks and feels welcoming.

Lighting can be another creative tool in marking out individual spots within an open-plan living space. The whole area should be equipped with powerful general illumination for when the space is being used in its entirety, but ceiling lights should be zoned, so that while activity areas like the kitchen and main dining table are kept bright, those in the sitting zone may be atmospherically dimmed. Consider arranging halogen downlights in a circle above a sofa or adding a dramatic pendant light above a dining table. Quiet zones will need at least one decent reading lamp, whether floor-standing or wall-mounted. Also consider lights that look good glowing in the gloom—modern illuminated acrylic cubes, a loop of flickering garland lights, or a wall-mounted lamp with colored LEDs, for example.

The most effective open-plan spaces look cohesive and are conceived with a single color scheme, highlighted with accent shades. In a modern space, it can be fun to pick hot colors for busy zones and use cool monochrome ones to designate quiet areas. For a more muted variation, settle on a single shade, then use a middle tone of it on the wall adjacent to a kitchen area, say, and a darker, more inviting one for sitting-room upholstery. Changes in flooring—both visual and textural—can also offer subtle delineation. Plan glossy, hard floors—concrete, limestone, or tiles, for example—in high-traffic activity zones and deliberately contrast them with more welcoming and tactile floorboards or rubber in a sitting area. Alternatively, an abstract rug or an inset glass floor can provide a useful focus for grouping furniture.

OPPOSITE PAGE **It's important to supply area-specific task lights as well as general illumination. Take inspiration from the architectural style. In this converted factory, with its dramatically high ceilings, huge pendant lights dangle over the dining table, while a giant angled floor lamp pools light onto a reading chair. By day, the chosen styles dominate the space and create visual drama; by night they fulfill a very practical role.**

BELOW **In a smaller open-plan space, with a single sitting zone, aim for flexibility. In this tiny apartment, the armchair may be faced toward the dining table for sociable evenings, pulled up to the fire, or turned away from the table to face a floor-to-ceiling bookcase. It's worth working out potential layouts on a scale plan before installing furniture. Extra flexibility is easily achieved by using furniture on castors.**

It is these structures that can make the difference between a frustrating lack of peace at home and a happy mix of privacy and sociability.

There's a reassuring solidity about a conventional house with its ordinary walls and doors. We can choose to be enclosed within a room with the door shut, keeping out extraneous noise and people. Or we may leave internal doors open, letting in light and the babble of family life. Yet these fixed boundaries are changing. With our predilection for altering living spaces—from creating open-plan and double-height areas to connecting bathrooms—privacy at home is often compromised. The *Oxford English Dictionary* defines partition as "division into parts; structure separating two such parts," and it is these structures that can make the difference between a frustrating lack of peace at home and a happy mix of privacy and sociability.

Of course, partitions aren't new: they have been eternally popular, from traditional Japanese sliding doors, employed to divide sleeping and living spaces, to the decorative freestanding screens used throughout Europe across the centuries. In more recent times, fixed partitions gained a disreputable image, conjuring up visions of flimsy wall-divisions in cheap housing. Today's architects and designers have revived partitioning as a vital way of screening and cutting down noise in open-plan spaces. Even better, partitions can be used to make a strong decorative statement in an enticing array of new materials. Depending on the style you choose—stationary or movable—you can use them to support ever-changing configurations of space and privacy.

RIGHT **The most effective forms of partitioning offer flexibility. With its combination of folding doors, glass partition walls, and simple curtains, this romantic bedroom can be completely closed off for an intimate retreat or remain a sociable part of the mezzanine.**

partitions

ABOVE LEFT AND RIGHT **Closed, glass sliding doors offer total privacy; partially open, they allow a connection with spaces beyond.**

LEFT **Glass paneling and built-in cupboards provide a solid, yet light-diffusing partition between two halves of a large room.**

OPPOSITE PAGE **A plain wood door, set with horizontal grooves, marks a clear division between public and private areas on the ground floor.**

First, it's vital to decide why you need partitioning. Are you looking to divide "public" and private areas at home—between a hall and bedrooms, for example? Or is it needed to screen off a section of a large double room or to enclose a room-within-a-room? Because partitions are architectural structures, these are questions that are best answered early in the building process. Solid, fixed partitions will affect space-planning everywhere else, as well as dictating the style and even the color of a space. Movable partitions, from a sliding door to a screen on wheels, are easier to add later, but every form of partitioning requires a well-considered financial outlay. Even if you are not using an architect while doing construction work, it can be well worth hiring a professional for a one-off consultation. Architects are trained to think in 3-D, so they will be able to suggest partitioning ideas that seamlessly integrate into the "skin" of the room.

As for possible materials and types of partitioning, do your market research early—it makes the decision-making process easier. As a starting point, amass tear-sheets from interior magazines that depict unusual ideas. Cast the net wide and look at potential industrial materials, which can be striking in a home setting. Investigate office partitioning, which may be adapted (it is often specifically designed to shut out unwanted noise). Also look at modern blind catalogs—many offer sliding wall panels—in addition to home improvement stores, which will stock a host of doors and panels. There are also the options of going direct to a specialized manufacturer for made-to-measure glass doors, or finding a good carpenter, who will assist in designing wooden partitions.

In its most basic form, partitioning is achieved with a humble pair of doors. Firmly shut, they provide a physical, noise-controlling barrier; left open, they allow natural light to flow. Double doors are ideal to partition a hall and adjacent living space, to link a series of rooms, or to separate a corridor leading to a private study or sitting room from an open-plan space. In a knocked-through living room, they can usefully mark a division between activity and quiet zones. Double doors have the added advantage of imparting drama: left ajar they offer enticing glimpses of the room beyond.

ABOVE **With its mix of pivoting doors, glass walls, and solid partitions, this flat delivers privacy where it's needed, screening the entrance to the bathroom. Glass panels at ceiling height maintain the visual theme.**

RIGHT **The key zones of kitchen and dining area have no solid division, and the glass walls allow light from the kitchen window to permeate the entire space.**

OPPOSITE PAGE **Dual themes are at work In the bedroom: pivoting translucent panels add privacy, while brightly colored walls enhance the sense of enclosure.**

Scale them taller than conventional door height, and they will also give a trompe l'oeil illusion of grandeur, enhancing the proportions of a small room.

Sliding doors, either singly or as a pair, offer a contemporary variation on the theme. They are particularly good in a modern space, as they look streamlined. It's a matter of personal choice whether they are designed to disappear into a concealed pocket within the wall or stack as sections to the side. But because they don't need to sweep through a curve, as conventional doors do, they are the best option if space is tight.

Pivoting doors form a particularly dramatic partition. A single door or pair of doors set within a wide aperture in the wall perform the same function as double doors. But scaled up, from floor to ceiling, and used in multiple sections, they also create a stunning, flexible wall.

Decisions on materials and style should be dictated by your initial reasons for choosing partition doors. Doors made from solid wood or laminated acoustic glass, which includes a noise-reducing membrane, are best for acoustic control. For privacy, choose sand-blasted or acid-etched glass, as it lets through light but remains translucent. Acrylic and corrugated plastic won't keep out noise, but offer very attractive translucence. To define a space lacking architectural detailing, or to make a strong decorative statement, consider composite-board doors, which may be laser-cut with a pattern or paneled with moldings.

In a property with period architectural detailing, by contrast, it's vital to design doors that blend seamlessly with existing architectural styles, so a classic painted wood or iron frame fitted with clear glass may be the best solution. In a modern space, where the emphasis is on overlapping vertical planes, doors should be in a minimal style, such as frameless glass or flush wood. In a converted industrial building, proportions should be scaled up to match high ceilings and a spacious floor area. Metal doors, from stainless steel to zinc, look appropriate in such a setting.

In a more conventional home, where walls have been knocked down between two rooms to create an open-plan space, fixed sections of wall are a better partition option. Acting as narrow, floor-to-ceiling divisions, they provide natural corners for seclusion and can block unsightly views. A builder will be able to tell you which wall sections need to be left in place because they have a load-bearing function, but others may be added for space-defining purposes or to create drama. A sculptural curved wall added to an open-plan space, for example, leads the visitor enticingly around the corner, while an angled partition wall between an open-plan living room and the door to the bathroom creates a discreet barrier and prevents views directly into the private room.

In smaller spaces that have been opened up but which still lack ample natural daylight, it's vital that partitions, however narrow, are designed to allow plenty of light flow. In an industrial-style space, glass bricks are a good choice. Or consider punctuating a solid partition with an internal window at eye level to create views between rooms, yet maintain a sense of seclusion. If noise is a problem, plain laminated glass will offer a small amount of insulation. For particularly dramatic glass-panel options, consult a specialized glass supplier. One relatively new type on the market is glass with light-emitting diodes (LEDs), which illuminate the glass with tiny pinpricks of light.

In an open-plan space, there is invariably the need for some subtle sectioning off. In a bachelor pad, for example, screening may be required for the bed area if visitors are present. Or a space may need to be configured so that a section of living area can be entirely closed off to create an impromptu spare room or a work zone. In all cases, floor-to-ceiling sliding panels are the best way to section off a private space as and when needed. If the panels are to be used regularly, invest in the best

RIGHT AND FAR RIGHT **A glass wall is an ingenious way of creating a division without sacrificing light flow. But it also has the effect of "framing" the room, so you will need to keep the contents scrupulously neat. To heighten the dramatic effect, consider painting the back wall in a dark color. To retain a sense of connection between the enclosure and the space beyond, keep flooring continuous.**

track mechanism you can afford, installing tracks to the ceiling and floor. Sliding panels chosen to create privacy should be opaque, and there are many decorative options. In addition to solid wood and glass, consider composite coated with wood veneer, leather, horsehair, wallpaper, or paint. Heavy-duty canvas stretched across a steel frame is inexpensive and versatile, and the canvas may be painted.

In spaces where you want to create a visual division, but where noise control and privacy are less of an issue, try a more informal style of partition. Blind companies will make sliding wall screens to measure in a variety of fabrics, from opaque to translucent, including such exciting options as colored vinyl. If you want a softer, more romantic look, try suspending fabric panels at random intervals from the ceiling, or hang them from a narrow steel suspension wire anchored in the ceiling. In a funky apartment, a cascade of beaded strands or a chain-link curtain will create a similarly effective division.

Within an open-plan space, it is always bedrooms and bathrooms that require the most careful planning. Committed loft-dwellers may argue that it's OK to have even the bathtub on view and that to partition it off spoils the ethos of open-plan living, but most of us prefer to have a private bathroom, however tiny, tucked in one corner and behind solid walls. As for sleeping, there's nothing cozy (or private) about a bed that is in full view of the main living space. Unless you are scrupulously neat, visitors won't want to see your bedroom mess. And anyway, it's far more comfortable, and less drafty, to fall asleep within an enclosed area.

But although it's necessary to separate off bedrooms and bathrooms, blocking off a conventional room with solid walls and a door can look clumsy within an airy, flexible, open-plan space. So be imaginative. A glass-walled bedroom lets in plenty of light by day and adds an intriguing private/public dimension. A wall of structural glass should be constructed using laminated glass, if it is contained within a frame, or toughened glass,

which is five times stronger than ordinary clear glass. To provide screening from within the bedroom, think about floor-to-ceiling sheer curtains, Venetian blinds, or shades in a bright color. Alternatively, consider acid-etched glass in squares or stripes, which will allow tantalizing glimpses in and out.

For an opaque bedroom or bathroom "box," consider composite, plywood (left natural or painted), or wood veneers. To ensure a cohesive look throughout the entire living area, it's a good idea to echo the chosen material in another part of the space, too, as a section of wall paneling, perhaps, or on cabinet doors. Don't forget ventilation. It goes without saying that the "room" should be positioned so it has a window, to let in light and air. But also consider vertical or horizontal "slits" in the bedroom walls, building walls that stop just short of the ceiling, or puncturing them with circular holes. For a fun touch, add colored lighting within the bedroom: at night the "box" will glow enticingly.

OPPOSITE PAGE, LEFT AND RIGHT **This city apartment uses a variety of devices to partition off different zones within the open-plan space. Totally enclosed, the intimate "box" bedroom offers complete privacy for its owner. Painted white inside and out, its exterior blends easily with the structural columns, while the inside feels cool and calm. Waist-height slits allow for ventilation, and at night—when the room is illuminated—the openings cast dramatic patterns into the living space beyond.**

ABOVE LEFT **Neatly sandwiched next to the bedroom, the galley kitchen is separated from the main living area using color, rather than physical divisions. The bright green walls clearly define it as an activity zone.**

ABOVE RIGHT **To enhance the impact of the vertical partitions, the owner has played with horizontal levels, too. From the main living area, it's a step up to go to bed, and—with low ceilings already in place—the "box" feels even more intimate.**

mezzanines

The attraction of a mezzanine floor is that it offers a connection with the main open-plan space, yet is an autonomous room.

It might be argued that a mezzanine is the ultimate private place. Suspended midway between ceiling and ground-floor level, affording a bird's-eye view onto the living zone downstairs, it promises a contained space for relaxing, while putting a physical distance between its occupants and the ebb and flow of daily activity below. Increasing numbers of people choose to live in converted industrial spaces, from former schools to factories, which inevitably have high ceilings. It makes sense in such properties, most of which are open plan, to divide up the residence vertically, using a mezzanine both to extend the existing floor area and to define the voluminous space. But by far the best advantage of such a new floor, of course, is that it affords an enticing means of escape.

The type of mezzanine you choose will depend in part on the size of the building and how daring you wish to be architecturally. In a very large space, with ceilings that may rise to as high as twenty feet and a capacious floor area, a substantial mezzanine is possible. It may extend across a good third or even half of the floor below, supported on pillars or the surrounding walls, and accommodate a number of rooms and even a corridor. In a more modestly sized space, the mezzanine may contain a single-function room. This is a good choice in a loft conversion that has plenty of height but restricted floor space (often the result of a larger warehouse having been divided up into many smaller units). In its simplest form, a mezzanine is a basic raised platform.

LEFT **The most successful mezzanine arrangement boasts a mix of light sources. Here, a double-height window and an inset upstairs window bring in plenty of sunshine, while the glass balustrade guarantees good light flow. Plenty of ceiling lights illuminate the space at night.**

Surprisingly, perhaps, a mezzanine can be a very cost-effective way of adding a private retreat, though of course the price will be affected by choice of materials, its size, and the complexity of the structure. Don't embark on planning and design without employing a structural engineer, who will advise on crucial structural aspects, such as how the mezzanine will be supported, accessed, and built, and will also supply drawings and calculations for the approval of building inspectors. An architect, though not strictly necessary, can bring a dynamic visual and spatial approach to the function and look of a mezzanine floor, tailoring it to your needs.

First, crystallize why you want a mezzanine and how it will be used. In a busy, open-plan family space, it can be the ideal way to create a book-lined adult sitting room—without a toy in sight—well away from the main kitchen/dining/living area. Access by tiny children can be restricted with the use of a stair gate and by older children with a firm house rule! A mezzanine floor devoted to bedrooms and bathrooms is the best solution for keeping a firm division between public downstairs and private family zones upstairs. If one person works from home, a study is very nicely housed on a separate level. A tiny platform is the answer if a retreat is required only occasionally—think of a sleeping platform for impromptu guests or a computer desk in the eaves.

Exactly where you position the mezzanine is also a crucial decision as it affects both low- and high-level living. You will need to think about how to keep it private from people looking up from the ground floor, as well as what occupants will see if they look down into the main living area. It's not very restful, for example, to view a messy kitchen from above, so it may be a good idea to arrange the cooking area beneath a mezzanine floor. In a double-height space, the underside of a mezzanine creates a lower ceiling height, perfect for a cozy sitting or dining nook. Decide, too, if the visual "wow-factor" is important. If so, the mezzanine should be planned as a dominant architectural feature, taking center stage in the space and accentuated by a design-statement staircase.

Of course, it's vital for the new area to be as comfortable as the rest of the living space: the room must be worth the ascent to a higher level and cozy to sit in. As a rule of thumb, the ceiling should be at least eight feet high—providing ample room for an adult to stand up—otherwise, the space will feel claustrophobic. Decent natural light is also crucial. A mezzanine that is set into a double-height space, with an accompanying double-height window, won't necessarily require separate windows, but you may wish to put internal windows into a back wall. However, a bedroom will need exterior windows—to give views, fresh air, and sunlight. You will also need to plan efficient ventilation and heating. Because hot air

ABOVE **Give plenty of attention to the view upstairs. Concentrate as much on the upper echelons of a double-height wall as on the ground-floor level. In this new-build house, a door from the main living area—and seen from the mezzanine—has been elongated to balance the tall proportions of the space. A wall alcove, cleverly set at mid-height, also looks appropriate at both levels.**

OPPOSITE PAGE **Careful furniture choices and arrangement will help maximize the potential of a compact second floor. An L-shaped sofa looks more streamlined than several armchairs. Here, the sofa faces away from the double-height space, which makes the area feel cozy. Stackable furniture, like the nesting tables, is also a boon in a confined space.**

rises, a mezzanine may require electrically operated roof windows, or at the very least a ceiling fan, to prevent stuffiness, especially in the summer. A separate heat source, such as a radiator, may be necessary for mezzanine bedrooms in winter.

A room that is a part of, yet separate from, a large-scale double-height space requires especially careful furnishing and decorating. It's tricky, for example, to make a room feel intimate if it is suspended beneath an arched or sloping ceiling of vast proportions. To bring a ceiling height down, consider lining it with tongue-and-groove paneling or painting it a darker color. (By contrast, paint a very low ceiling—and surrounding walls—white, or at least use gloss paint to enhance space.) If the ceiling is high, choose scaled-up furniture that has enveloping curved or corner features, such as L-shaped modular upholstered furniture or a canopied bed. Low-ceilinged rooms will benefit from a streamlined daybed or floor cushions to enhance the laid-back mood.

Although a lateral open-plan space should have a universal decorative scheme—one that coheres whichever way you view the room—you can bend the rules a little with colors and textures in a mezzanine. If the overall living space is light and white, then add darker furnishings, a wall lined with books, or a brightly painted back wall to give a more intimate feel to the mezzanine. Use occasional lamps, in addition to the shared ceiling lights, to make the space seem homey, and—if the main space has predominantly hard, glossy surfaces—add warming textures, such as carpet on the floor, deep-pile upholstery, and cozy cushions and throws.

Part of the attraction of a mezzanine floor is that it offers a visual and auditory connection with the main open-plan space, yet is an autonomous room. On the one hand, it can be useful to keep abreast of what is happening downstairs (especially if you have children) and even chat to family, making it positively sociable. The disadvantage, of course, is that noise travels up. (So do food smells, but a top-quality cooking ventilator will take care of those.) So ask yourself whether it is privacy or noise control that matters most. Your answer will directly influence your choice of style of enclosure. Every mezzanine must have at least a guardrail, if not more solid floor-to-ceiling structures, to keep it safe.

If privacy is a prime concern, then concentrate on screening that both controls noise and restricts views from below. A large mezzanine housing

OPPOSITE PAGE AND ABOVE **Snug and whimsical, this vibrant bedroom is quite different in mood from its industrial, converted warehouse surroundings. Yet it perfectly exemplifies the decorative freedom that a mezzanine room— be it a boudoir, playroom, or study —can afford. Inner curtains keep the hot pink scheme a surprise from visitors down below, but once you're inside, the riot of pattern and color from textiles, rag rug, and handpainted mural create an instant mood change. Decorated with pretty lamps and a chandelier, plus reflective gloss paint, the bedroom comes into its own as a nighttime retreat. But the glass walls and simple unlined curtains mean the room can be used by day as well.**

LEFT AND BELOW **Cleverly appointed in the central section of a city loft apartment, this snug sitting room is firmly connected to the ground-floor living area, yet retains a pleasing sense of seclusion. Floor-to-ceiling glass folding doors can be shut to reduce noise without cutting down the flow of light. To the rear of the room, pivoting windows let in more light and ventilation, and provide a bird's-eye view down to the entrance hall.**

RIGHT **The mezzanine floor offers an enticing mix of seclusion and sociability. Because you can lean over a balustrade (or look through it), make sure the furniture arrangement looks good from above as well as below.**

FAR RIGHT **Pay attention to lighting for stairs, any adjacent landings, and the mezzanine itself. Lights should be on a dimmer, so you can control mood at night or add extra illumination on a dull day.**

family bedrooms may be constructed with a glass-walled corridor, while the rooms themselves may have solid walls. The glass wall will offer some noise reduction, while assisting light flow and maintaining the drama of a double-height space. (A glass wall may also need to be fireproofed.) If there is just one bedroom overlooking the main space, separated from the staircase by a landing, a simpler solution will be to put in sliding or conventional double doors—made from translucent acid-etched glass or solid or veneered wood. Alternatively, devise a "wall" of opaque panels to divide the vertical plane between mezzanine and main space. These must be stationary up to waist height, but may be partially, or completely, folded back by day, depending on how much light and privacy you require.

For those who relish the physical separation of a mezzanine floor, but want it to look—and be—part of the open-plan whole, then choose light-enhancing glass or open metal balustrades for safety rather than privacy. On any raised platform, it's vital to provide a balustrade to prevent people (and especially children) from falling off. Your structural engineer will advise on the correct height, but three feet is a good rule of thumb. The balustrade will be on view from downstairs, so choose a design that fits well with the prevailing architectural mood. Stainless-steel bars, tensioned stainless-steel cables, and toughened glass are all chic, contemporary choices and don't impede views or light flow. On a small mezzanine, you could even consider a laminated glass floor so that a desk or sitting area appears to "float" within the bigger space.

Just as sitting aloft in a double-height space feels intimate, so should the ascent feel special and even adventurous. However, if the mezzanine is big enough to be classed as an extra room, access must be deemed

LEFT **This family space has been expertly planned with the parents' bedroom above the kitchen and the child's room sensibly adjacent to the ground-floor living space. With its cut-away sections, the wooden "wall" allows for both communication and valuable peace and quiet.**

OPPOSITE PAGE, TOP LEFT AND BOTTOM **A well-considered mix of lighting options is especially important for a bedroom. To control natural light, wall panels are hinged at the upper level, so may be folded back to allow in more sunshine. The resulting apertures afford a great view outdoors through double-height windows on the opposite wall. Side windows are also screened with solid folding panels. For ambient electric light at night in the room itself, or to create a dramatic feature seen from the ground floor, there are inset floor lights.**

OPPOSITE PAGE, TOP RIGHT **In this restricted space, it made sense to choose a narrow, steep, partially enclosed staircase. Drama is focused on the floor-to-ceiling wood-veneer walls, which feature shelf storage on either side.**

sufficiently practical to meet fire regulations (your structural engineer will advise). In a double-height space, where the scale is bold and the volume large, the choice will be between a dramatic, statement staircase and a concealed stairwell. But a basic platform, used only occasionally as a sleeping zone, is perfectly well served with a sturdy ladder or accessed via a simple staircase constructed from big wooden cubes. A ladder should be securely and vertically anchored to the wall rather than awkwardly projecting into the living space.

If you choose a dramatic staircase as access, you won't need to look far for inspiration, as the designer staircase is the star of our times. Consider cantilevered treads emerging from the wall, a hanging staircase suspended on cables from beneath the mezzanine, or—good in a more confined space—a spiral or helical staircase. Glass treads or a glass balustrade work well in an open-plan area since they don't block views or light, and may be lit with light-emitting-diodes (LEDs), providing a particularly dramatic look if the main space is in darkness. By contrast, if the mezzanine is a truly private zone, keep the staircase tucked out of sight. A vertical or gently curved flight of stairs, fully enclosed by walls on both sides, feels particularly intimate.

If an attic remodel feels like an extravagance, it's worth remembering that it will cost considerably less than moving.

Called an attic or a garret, the roof space beneath the eaves of a house has romantic connotations. Traditionally the place where an artist honed his craft, these days it is often the first spot to which we turn when in search of an extra room. It has much to recommend it: with its sloping ceilings, an attic provides a cosy environment that feels enclosing and private. Situated at the top of the house, there's no chance of annoying footfalls above, so peace is guaranteed. Even better, it can be a room flooded with daylight, providing attractive sky views. For a few quiet hours, city-dwellers may kid themselves that the urban landscape doesn't even exist.

But before rushing to create a tranquil attic eyrie, it's crucial to assess the potential of your home. A successful attic conversion is dependent on sufficient breadth and height of roof space. A period property with a traditionally sloping roof usually offers the greatest possibilities, though not every house has a tall enough cavity. (A good rule of thumb is that the central head height should be at least eight feet.) Modern properties are often harder to convert. In the 1960s, the prevailing method of roof construction changed, from rafters and purlins to trussed rafters. The latter are trickier to remove without affecting the roof support, though these days some specialized attic-conversion companies will tackle these, too. Some new-built houses are even supplied with a semi-constructed roof space.

RIGHT **Children and teenagers will love the freedom of an attic bedroom retreat. They won't mind sloping walls or a restricted ceiling height, and an attic room affords peace and quiet for doing homework. Built-in beds and simple, cheerful furnishings increase the appeal of this space.**

attics

If an attic remodel feels like an extravagance, it's worth remembering that it will cost considerably less than moving. And with today's fluid family arrangements (children who return home after college, elderly parents) crucially affecting privacy at home, it's worth investing in an extra room before the need gets too pressing. So if you're moving into a new property, do the work now, not in five years' time. The addition of living space will radically affect the configuration of the entire family home: even if you don't use the attic itself as a private retreat, you could shift a teenager's bedroom up there to free up space for a longed-for study.

An attic conversion doesn't need to be a particularly complex building job, but it makes sense to call in the experts. Many specialized conversion companies will mastermind the entire project, but if you are confident in design and detailing, it's a job that can be completed using a competent carpenter and advice from a structural engineer. For a major attic conversion, or for creative input, use an architect. Professionals will negotiate any local regulations. Permission may not be required unless the property is in a historical zone and, say, a dormer window is to be added (which alters the exterior look of the house). But if a room is to be slept in, it is classified as a habitable space, and it must satisfy local regulations.

Long before planning design, decide whom the attic room is for. In a family, an attic bedroom offers ultimate peace for adults: no one else has a reason to go up there, unless invited. Precisely because the room will be planned from scratch, it's the ideal opportunity to get a tailor-made bedroom with perfectly sited heating and lighting. An attic room is also a

OPPOSITE PAGE, TOP **However small, an attic bathroom will always be an asset. Sharply sloping ceilings may dictate a tub rather than a shower. In a compact space, keep surfaces cohesive: here, the wooden bath enclosure, wall, and floor look streamlined and cozy.**

OPPOSITE PAGE, BOTTOM LEFT **Even if the space is tiny, it's a good idea to put in a washbasin. Play with scale: here, a large basin, with sleek designer faucets, tricks the eye into thinking the space is bigger than it is.**

OPPOSITE PAGE, BOTTOM RIGHT **Don't rule out a spare attic bedroom just because ceiling height is restricted—more time will be spent lying down than standing up! To prevent a sloping roof from feeling claustrophobic, insert big skylights, so there is plenty of sunlight and ventilation, and keep to pale decorative tones.**

LEFT **Don't put off an attic conversion just because there is not enough height for built-in storage. In this steeply pitched bedroom, architectural features prompt new solutions such as the quirky shirt hanger and low-level drawer storage.**

A properly converted attic room deserves the same decorative attention as any room in the house, so don't skimp on budget or style.

RIGHT AND OPPOSITE PAGE, LEFT **A conversion done on a tight budget can still look fresh and pretty. Invest in good planning and building work now to create the shell. You can add more expensive finishes and furniture at a later date. Save on custommade carpentry by choosing thrift-store furniture in small sizes, and add a basic wood-plank floor, which can be painted with gloss floor paint now and carpeted later. Keep things simple in a budget room: pale tones, accessorized with simple fabrics, such as denim and muslin, are peaceful and welcoming.**

OPPOSITE PAGE, RIGHT **If the architecture requires an unusual niche, then use such a feature as a prompt for furniture layout. The low enclosing walls and skylight in this bedroom create a perfect space for the bed.**

brilliant option for a grown-up child needing separate living and sleeping space. Depending on the size of the attic, there may be space for several small rooms or one big one. Either way, when installing a bedroom it's a good idea to consider adding bathroom facilities. In a master bedroom, make it a luxurious bathroom or shower. Even in a tiny room, plan for a wall-mounted sink.

For those working from home, or in need of occasional cozy study space, an attic is equally appealing. The smallest of rooms comfortably accommodates a desk, chair, and storage unit. Commission a carpenter to line and fill the lowest sections of the under-eaves cavity with purpose-built cupboards, or choose pre-assembled doors from a home improvement store. Good storage is vital, whatever the room function. It's hard to break with the traditional belief that an attic is for accumulating stuff, so either learn to live without clutter or plan concealed storage for keeping seasonal clothes and the like out of view. A properly converted attic room deserves the same decorative attention as any other room in the house, so don't skimp on budget or style.

Concentrate on technical issues in tandem with the design. It's vital to decide early on the finishes and hardware that will be required, so that the correct infrastructure can be put into place. Steel support beams will be needed, particularly in older properties, where the floor joists will have been inserted for ceiling support only and not for a new floor above. If you're planning a limestone-floored bathroom, for example, you should check whether additional structural support would be required. You may also need to upgrade the water tank and put in a system that can supply adequate water pressure.

Electricity and central heating are easily extended from the main house supply, but ensure there are enough outlets for comfort, and bear in mind that a home study may require a phone or ethernet jack for the computer as well. Good ventilation and heating are equally important: because it's under the eaves, an attic can be too hot in summer and freezing in winter. So in addition to roof windows, install ventilation panels or an electric ceiling fan, which will add atmosphere. There should also be enough radiators or vents. Can your existing boiler cope with the additional services?

OPPOSITE PAGE **Be imaginative when planning the ascent to an attic. Simple yet dramatic, this crucifix points the way upstairs, and fills an otherwise dead space.**

FAR LEFT **Nothing beats the impact of a steep, straight staircase: consider adding a skylight directly above it to flood light down and illuminate a naturally dark space.**

LEFT **A basic ladder can become a strong, decorative statement. With its wooden treads and steel uprights, this one is matched to the flooring and carpentry.**

The roof windows you choose for an attic will make or break its decorative potential. As a good rule of thumb, windows should be ten to twenty percent of the attic floor area in size to provide adequate daylight. But the style you choose should be based on different criteria. If you are after an energizing workspace or a tranquil sky view from the bed, large roof windows are the solution. But in a period property, a traditional cast-metal skylight is preferable (it may even be required by the local building code). Dormer windows will add head height, but provide a more conventional-looking and less inspiring room. Dormers may also need to be approved and create a more complex, and therefore more expensive, building project. It is, perhaps, the window coverings that most crucially affect ambience. Steer clear of patterned and fancy designs, which will distract the eye; choose soothing solids instead. To control temperature and light, choose blackout blinds with aluminum backing to reduce heat gain and loss. Some companies sell exterior awnings, which prettily filter the sunlight.

Decoratively speaking, it can be fun to plan an attic room in direct contrast to the rest of the house. You can afford to be indulgent: because of its location, this is the one room where the decorative scheme cannot be glimpsed from the stairway, so it doesn't have to match. If you are after an industrial-style workspace, consider keeping aged beams and the rafters exposed and adding a reclaimed wood floor. Alternatively, you might wish to paint walls in a bright, funky shade in direct contrast to a neutral, well-considered scheme elsewhere. But for a truly tranquil and escapist bedroom, paint walls and floorboards white, with furnishings to match, so that attention rises upward to inspiring views of treetops and sky.

Don't forget the importance of good access. An attic room that will be used only occasionally is perfectly well served by a wall-mounted ladder, which will take up minimal floor space and offers a visual sense of intrigue. An extra-tall ladder, perhaps in steel or painted to match the wall color, looks particularly dramatic. For a room used on a daily basis, a proper staircase is essential. Specialized stores offer a good choice of vertical staircases, as well as more traditional spiral options. But for a seamless finish, it is worth considering a custom-built staircase, which may be blended with the existing stair or designed to inspire. Zinc treads, an illuminated glass staircase, or a cantilevered stair will make the ascent as thrilling as the private room itself.

escape outdoors

It's an odd paradox that once we're settled at home, we often feel at our most relaxed when looking back out through the windows onto the busy world we've escaped. As cozy as they are to retreat behind (and we should also screen them for privacy) windows provide us with a crucial link between the sanctuary of home and the great outdoors. They are powerful tools for creating ambience and a good mood, as well as offering a visual escape to the inspiring natural world.

Sitting outside in your garden or on a sunny deck, you can read, sunbathe, or relax in a way that's impossible on the beach or in the park. So however tiny your living quarters, it's worth buying, begging, or borrowing precious square feet outside for a small balcony, a roof terrace, or a patch of urban garden. What matters is that it is enclosed and soulful, a place you are as happy to sit in alone as sharing with friends.

An escape outdoors can also mean creating a private place at the end of the garden. Having a dedicated hut outdoors is the city-dweller's equivalent of a tent in a field, a quiet garden plot, or an afternoon fishing from a boathouse. At one with the big outdoors—but still in touch (if we choose to use a telephone), a secluded garden room or a gazebo is perhaps the private place most of us would choose.

To get the best from good windows at home, earmark one or two for creating a quiet relaxation zone.

However tranquil our surroundings at home, it is often the natural elements outside—a leafy view, a snatch of birdsong, a glimpse of blue sky—that imbue us with the deepest sense of peace. By turning toward a window just for a few moments, our backs to the domestic scene, we can escape everyday activity and noise and take pleasure in the natural (or urban) world outside. And that's not all. Because windows let in light, air, and warmth, they are powerful tools for creating ambience at home. Yet despite their importance, we all too often take them for granted, swathing them in unnecessary window dressings or failing to open them to fresh air. When buying a new home, we may not even notice the crucial view from each window.

Happily, the vogue for large windows is growing, championed by contemporary architects in both new-built modern homes and modest extensions. If the trend is inspired, in part, by the glass-box style of twentieth-century Modernist homes, it is fueled, too, by our ever-increasing desire to be in touch with the natural world. And "bringing the outside in" aren't just buzzwords: increasingly we strive to blend exterior spaces with our interior environment, by merging inside and outside flooring, furniture, and views. Windows are part of that crucial link. In a modern building, good styles include floor-to-ceiling sliding windows, frameless picture windows, or a wall of glass. In period properties, classic French doors or a tall sash window perform a similar function.

PREVIOUS PAGE **A favorite spot to sit and think may change seasonally as flowers bloom and die away. Keep a comfortable (folding wooden or plastic) chair by the back door, then pick the prettiest place to sit.**

RIGHT **A great view calls for minimal "dressing," so keep things simple. In this new-built house, rooms have been planned to take in nearby glimpses of a lake and sailing boats. The fresh, light curtains are made from sail material.**

windows

Fabulous though it is to enjoy unimpeded views, the flip side of big windows is that everyone else can see in—and at night, especially in the city, the home can become a spectacular goldfish bowl. If the interior of your home is rigorously ordered and beautifully lit at night, and you enjoy an exhibitionist streak, all well and good. For the rest of us, there's the need to solve the problem of how to enjoy views out without the whole world looking in. Of course, there are myriad ways to screen windows from the inside, but think of the bigger picture. For those contemplating a new-built project, large windows are ideally placed to the rear or side of the house, assuming the yard is not overlooked. If they must go in the front, consider specialized glass that is reflective on the street side.

To get the best from good windows at home, earmark one or two for creating a quiet relaxation zone. If the window is full height, pick furniture that, as well as providing comfort, has an attractive outline, as it will be silhouetted against the window. Think of retro chairs or a slim recliner rather than an over-stuffed sofa. In a period property, a low sash window may require a low-slung chaise longue, while a small square casement window may be just the right height to afford good views when you're seated at a desk. The furniture arrangement of the entire room should allow for uninterrupted glimpses from every angle in the space.

Remember that how much you see from the window matters less than what you see. If you have the opportunity to install a new window (in a historic area, there will be constraints), take time to work out the most inspiring view. Existing windows can be improved with simple measures: training a climbing plant up the wall and around the window or—if close to the treetops—adding a birdbox or strands of exterior tree lights. Don't assume that foliage growing too close to a window should be cut to improve light flow: lush greenery casts a particularly soothing, atmospheric light. If installing big windows in a back extension, remember that they will naturally frame what is going on outdoors. So make it worthy of the attention. Even a tiny garden must be kept neat and have plants that change seasonally—and you might want to add a soothing water feature.

FAR LEFT AND LEFT **The bigger the windows, the greater the potential to play decoratively with light, dark, and all nuances in between. The elements in this peaceful sitting room have been expertly planned to enhance those contrasts. While the glass-topped table and pale wood floor bounce back reflections, the darker upholstery and black rug add drama as daylight turns to dusk.**

However great the view, no window will be comfortable to sit in front of if it's too cold, too hot, or too noisy. There have been huge strides in the development of specialized glass, which, though not cheap, can solve all three problems. Low-emissivity glass reduces heat loss by retaining the temperature inside. There is also solar-control glass of many types, which prevents too much heat from coming into the building, and acoustic glass, which effectively bounces sound off the window and is more effective than double- or even triple-glazing.

A window must act as a physical, as well as a visual, link to the outside. A gentle breeze is very soothing, so make sure that windows open effectively to allow in fresh air. There's nothing more frustrating than a painted-up sash window or a stationary glass wall onto a garden, which can't be pushed aside. Any window that opens must be have appropriate locks for security and safety. Full-height windows at second-floor level or above should be flanked on the exterior by a three-foot-high balustrade. Alternatively, a tilt-and-turn mechanism allows the window to tilt into the room at ceiling height, letting in the breeze, while remaining safe at floor level. On a ground floor, floor-to-ceiling sliding windows are best planned to disappear into a concealed pocket to one side.

However lovely the exterior aspect, the majority of windows will require some formal screening. Most of us prefer to pull down the blinds or close curtains at night—certainly it is cozier in winter. But a well-chosen window treatment can also enhance a good view or improve a room's ambience.

FAR LEFT **If possible, add floor-to-ceiling French or sliding doors to a garden room to create an indoor-outdoor connection. With a table and stools close to the window, eating in this kitchen takes on an easy al fresco mood, even on cooler days.**

LEFT, TOP AND BOTTOM **There's great benefit in having at least a few trees close to home. For city dwellers, watching foliage fall in autumn then renew in spring, may be the only way to stay in touch with the seasons. Trees sound good, too: a window needs only to be ajar for you to hear peaceful rustling and birdsong. If you are able to add floor-to-ceiling windows, consider installing them upstairs rather than at ground level. You will get perfect views of tree and sky – the next best thing to a garden in an upper-level apartment.**

RIGHT **Plan decoration that works with, not against, the view. This room is suffused with green in summer and bronze in the fall, so a mix of neutrals, warm tones, and wood pieces looks effective. A city view, by contrast, may call for muted grays, blues, and white.**

THIS PAGE **Plan screening for every window on its own merits. A blind isn't always necessary if the room isn't overlooked. The street-facing window in this bedroom is obscured, while the forest-facing one is unadorned.**

RIGHT **As they are constantly back-lit by daylight, acid-etched glass panes create a particularly decorative focus in a room. Show off accessories with an attractive silhouette or experiment with colored-glass vases.**

FAR RIGHT **There's something very atmospheric about a shady room with its blinds half-drawn against the sun. To cultivate that mood, choose a Roman shade in a dense, dark fabric and add a bias border for definition.**

A well-chosen window treatment can enhance a good view or improve a room's ambience.

Blinds are now so popular that there are myriad options. In addition to conventional fabric styles, including Roman, roller, pull-up Swedish styles and traditional balloon shades, there are plantation shutters (from plain painted styles to leather-clad), Venetian blinds in wood, metal, or vinyl, acrylic folding shutters, and vertical louver blinds. Although blind manufacturing companies offer a huge choice, it's worth investigating other specialized sources, too. Conservatory suppliers offer plain, traditional options, including rattan blinds, which filter the sunlight attractively. Interior or textile designers may also offer innovative made-to-measure solutions, including pivoting fabric shutters or blinds in hi-tech, light-reflective, or knitted, sculptural materials.

As for curtains, unlined designs are best as they offer privacy without affecting the flow of light. Of course, style depends on the prevailing look in your room, but avoid fussy curtains: a rectangle of fabric with tie tops, a simple channel threaded onto suspension wire, or ones with eyelets are best. Natural fabrics are always appealing: think of voile, loose-weave linen, cotton, seersucker, or hemp. Stick to solids, so as not to distract from an attractive view outside, and neutral colors, such as white, beigo, or black. In a modern interior, high-tech voiles and sheers make an inspiring alternative. Often sporting unusual weaves, from a linen-mohair mix to meshed leather or funky colors shot through with metallic thread, they will cast muted, colorful shadows into the room, as well as shimmering attractively in the sun.

The tiniest balcony can make breakfast in the bedroom special, or provide a bird's-eye view of the world while you just sit and think.

It's good for us to escape outside at times of relaxation. Yet in today's busy world, we tend to switch off and stay indoors, preferring a cozy sofa to a blast of crisp air in the park. Try to counteract that instinct. By consciously preparing a quiet spot for peace and contemplation outdoors, however tiny, you are more likely to drag the yoga mat outside on a sunny morning or enjoy an al fresco early fall supper. For city-dwellers, there's always a fight to find decent exterior space. But even for those who live in the countryside, with a big property at their disposal, there is much to be said for creating a cozy, enclosed nook outdoors.

A balcony that leads, hotel-style, directly from a bedroom or sitting room is the easiest, and most user-friendly, link between outside and in. If your property already has a balcony, then celebrate. It is also comparatively straightforward to add a second-floor structure to a new extension, though much trickier to get planning permission to add one to a building in a historic area, since it alters the exterior character. The tiniest balcony, just big enough to hold a circular table and two chairs, can make breakfast in the bedroom special, or provide a bird's-eye view of the world while you just sit and think or read a book. Increase the ambience by training a climbing plant—and perhaps a string of exterior mini tree lights—around the safety balustrade or adding a pull-down canvas awning to provide protection from the sun.

RIGHT **A traditional covered porch offers the perfect exterior sanctuary. Sociably close to the street, and within shouting distance of the house, you can feel peaceful without being lonely. Furnish it with chairs for contemplation, or add a table and lighting for al fresco meals.**

balconies
& sitting areas

In a city apartment with no back yard, but which has available flat roof space adjacent to a room or on top of the property, consider a roof terrace. Because it is at high level, it will get plenty of sun and sky views, and because it will be less overlooked than a conventional yard, it will feel more private. Vital first steps to take include checking that you don't need planning permission and that the roof is robust enough to withstand the weight of people, flooring, and plants. Consult a structural engineer, who will advise on necessary loadbearing support and the correct height of a parapet. Many new buildings are constructed with roof-terrace use in mind and already have steel-beam support in place under the flat roof.

By its very nature, a roof terrace feels appropriately intimate, as it will have a compact floor area and requires high enclosing walls. Play up that mood by choosing attractive parapet materials. For an industrial look, pick metal mesh, bars, or tensioned stainless-steel cables. For a prettier, more conventional finish, painted tongue-and-groove willow fence panels, or a green-covered bamboo trellis, teamed with small trees and plants in giant tubs, are attractive. Think about clever lighting to maintain the mood at night: strings of Chinese

RIGHT **Choose plants that bloom at varying times, so there will always be something attractive to enjoy. Place evergreen shrubs around partition walls to conceal an urban view.**

OPPOSITE PAGE, LEFT **It's vital to consider the vista when planning a roof-top eyrie. Here, the neutral tones of wood and stone, and the angular contemporary furniture, blend neatly with the skyline.**

RIGHT **Consider alternatives to conventional garden furniture. This antique chair is easily dressed with upholstery pads on sunny days and is infinitely more comfortable than a deck chair.**

BELOW RIGHT **You can enjoy peace on a tiny balcony, even if it's overlooked by others. A fast-growing climbing plant, trained over a wood or metal frame, will rapidly provide shade and privacy.**

lanterns, plant spotlights, or candles in storm lanterns are all atmospheric choices. Many garden design companies specialize in small, custom-made urban gardens and roof terraces. Although they're not cheap, the extra space you reclaim outdoors will be well worth the cost, so think about booking a consultation.

Whether you have a balcony, roof terrace, deck or—in certain properties—a front porch, select dedicated furniture for the space. There's no point in creating a place for enjoying peace and quiet if you must drag out a chair from inside to do so. Decide if this is a spot for lying down, for eating a peaceful meal, or a bit of both. These days, garden furniture comes in almost as many style choices as interior pieces, either in weather-resistant hardwoods like teak, or in high-tech synthetic materials that withstand rain, cold, and sun damage. Do your research: the extra investment in quality pieces may be well worth it if cheap chairs fall apart after a single summer's outdoor use.

At least one pair of reclining chairs is essential. Classic wooden recliners or upholstered metal campaign chairs look good in a variety of settings, while modern options include bright polypropylene designer chairs and elegant white or silver mesh loungers. A built-in daybed is a good solution if space is really tight. Bench seating, with an upholstered pad to go on top, is great for one person lying down, or for accommodating several guests at an intimate party. (Design with a lift-up lid, and pads and cushions can be stored inside during the summer months.) A small chair and table are vital for al fresco meals. Even if there is a large family at home, necessitating a conventional eight-seater table, pick a quiet corner for a small table and pair of chairs, too. French metal café sets, a marble-topped antique pedestal table, or modern plastic choices are all appropriate. You could also consider adding a bamboo or pierced-metal folding screen for extra privacy.

For those with ample exterior space, it's still important to plan the garden to provide escapist nooks. A wide-open lawn, for example, may be screened at one end, using a fence of flower-covered trellis, planted bamboo, or tall shrubs, to create a separate area for sunbathing or reading. A small patch of enclosed lawn may be planted with scented herbs or strewn with wildflowers or seasonal daffodils or tulips as a quiet space to enjoy. A swing, made from a plank of wood and chains, could be hung from a solitary tree. Investigate the dark, moody space right at the end of the garden, too. Consider building a separate deck well out of earshot of the house—perhaps beneath mature trees—where you might suspend a hammock, add a canopy swing chair, or simply lie down to relax on thick rush mats.

OPPOSITE PAGE, TOP AND BOTTOM It's satisfying to have a quiet spot where you can eat outdoors, so plan for one in the garden, or on a balcony or roof terrace. You'll need to think about providing shade from the sun, as well as warmth in the fall—a patio heater is a good investment. While a parasol is the obvious screen against the sun, it's more soothing (and less intrusive) to use the natural shade from trees. Or choose a quirky alternative: this sun canopy (left) is made from sail material and flaps soothingly in the breeze.

ABOVE Inexpensive, lazy, and easy to install—provided you have the requisite two sturdy trees—the classic hammock is the ultimate outside retreat. You can't share it comfortably, so for a few hours at least, privacy is assured.

RIGHT Sometimes we just want a momentary escape. A swing isn't just for kids—suspend one from a tree, or the ceiling of a porch, and you will soon remember that life's pleasures are often the simplest ones.

sheds &
garden rooms

It's small wonder that more of us are choosing to add a garden structure to our homes to provide an extra spot to escape to.

Despite invariably mundane contents (paint cans, kids' bikes, tools), the conventional wooden shed has always had universal appeal. Often tucked at the end of the garden, its physical separation from the house promises a hint of privacy, while its scaled-down proportions appeal to the child in us all. Gardeners may see it as a sensible storehouse for seedlings and implements, but anyone in search of peace—from writers and artists to children or those working at home—regards it as the ultimate retreat from the domestic scene.

It's small wonder, then, that more of us are choosing to add a garden structure to our homes to provide an extra spot to escape to. For those who work regularly from home, a garden home office not only provides physical separation from a busy household, cutting down on noise and constant interruption, but the (albeit short) commute from home to garden marks an important emotional division between work and evening down-time. Family members with antisocial or "messy" hobbies— from photography (with a need for a darkroom) to home DJ-ing or portrait-painting—will also appreciate a zone that needn't be cleared up and in which creating noise isn't a problem. Then there are those who simply want a quiet spot for contemplation, taking in garden views and fresh air.

If a garden structure appeals, work out your available budget and do your research. The market is huge—offering every conceivable style, combination of materials, and interior fixtures—and quality

LEFT **In a small garden, where a shed is on view, it's important to choose an attractive style. Try to visually link it to the main house: this wooden shed has been painted a soothing soft gray, as have the French doors that lead from the kitchen to the garden.**

ABOVE **Choose a style with enough windows to allow for good ventilation and adequate light for reading. A large side window and glazed door provide the basics.**

ABOVE RIGHT **It's fun to camouflage a retreat among undergrowth, but when siting a shed, also take into consideration the direction of the sun and the potential views.**

RIGHT **A summer garden house should be furnished with light, easy furniture that can be removed for storage in winter. Create a casual mix of repainted junk finds and rattan pieces.**

and prices vary enormously. There will be decisions on whether to choose a modular unit, a made-to-measure design, or the humble do-it-yourself option, though even chain stores are offering increasingly sophisticated options. It's worth remembering that a garden office, fully wired and heated, will still cost substantially less than the price of adding a structural extension to the house. Also ask yourself who will use the new room. Try not to be too activity-specific: once the garden room is in place, you might decide to keep your quiet study in the body of the house while the kids move their den outdoors.

Where the garden escape will go, how much floor space it will occupy, and whether its presence is permitted by local building regulations are key questions that you will need to answer. As a rule of thumb, provided a garden structure isn't classed as a habitable structure, it doesn't require planning permission, but always check with your local authority before proceeding with your plans. If a specialized company is supplying the structure, they will advise on the regulations. It is generally accepted that a garden building should occupy no more than 50 percent of the exterior space, but small is good: you don't want a barn-like room, just a cozy retreat. Think about how the structure will look when glanced through the window. Decide whether to match the style to your own house or to go for a fantasy structure that will be just glimpsed between the trees.

The least sophisticated, but often most charming form of garden retreat is the humble wooden shed. Even the simplest will have a waterproof roof, a door, and a couple of windows (budget styles won't have glass). Finished in plain planking, inside and out, it will blend with garden foliage if the wood is treated and stained a natural shade.

To create a prettier focus, paint it a pale color, from French gray to white or blue. Certain paint selections offer exterior paints in a range of attractive muted and historical colors. It can be fun to furnish a shed with a reclining chair, side table, and even a hurricane lamp for evening sojourns, but try to pick weather-resistant garden furniture, which can survive damp conditions. It's fine to keep an upholstered piece outside during a short, hot spell, but don't expect it to endure the entire summer.

For something a little more magical, explore the garden structure market for unusual options. Specialized suppliers offer choices such as a traditional canvas teepee or a whimsical metal medieval-style tent frame, complete with fixed central chandelier and a weatherproof marine-canvas liner. These will appeal to grown-ups and children alike. Many companies offer traditional summerhouses. Designs may come with or without a porch, in a choice of window styles, from Gothic-leaded to sash, and with anything from real thatch to corrugated tin on the roof. But whether your garden retreat is simple or elaborately styled, remember that it is vital to capture sunshine and a good view. Some of the more sophisticated summerhouses come built onto a turntable, so in a big garden it's possible to follow the sun's rays.

The down side of a simple structure is that—once summer is over—it quickly becomes a chilly and damp place to be. So if you crave a year-round garden room, then it's essential to pick one that is wired for power and light, as well as a phone jack, a heat source, and weatherproof windows and doors. Your first port of call

OPPOSITE PAGE, TOP LEFT **In a large summerhouse, furnishings can be more permanent. A garden room is far removed from the main house, so you can afford to be experimental. Here, a cowhide rug and faux-fur cushions feel pampering and look trendy.**

OPPOSITE PAGE, BOTTOM LEFT **A dark-toned wood stain, rather than traditional garden greens and grays, looks subtle for a structure set deep into foliage. Paint the inside pure white or pale, muted tones to create a dramatic sense of contrast on arrival.**

OPPOSITE PAGE, RIGHT **For garden buildings close to the house, privacy remains a key issue. Shrubs or trees will go a long way to screening views in summer, but during the winter months you will also need curtains or blinds, which will help to reduce drafts.**

THIS PAGE **If space permits, add a day-bed or even a double bed to create the ultimate relaxation zone. Be indulgent with textures: plenty of cushions, a velvet or wool throw, and rugs are all great extras. And don't forget good overhead lighting, as well as lamps, for year-round use.**

ABOVE **If you're an avid gardener, site the outdoor retreat at the heart of the garden. This summerhouse is adjacent to herb borders, so access for their maintenance is easy—and the location is sweet-smelling.**

RIGHT **Take decorative inspiration from the garden. This storage cabinet is large enough to house plenty of books and equipment, and—with its organically inspired fretwork panels—blends with the surrounding foliage.**

OPPOSITE PAGE **Pay attention to decorative impact, both at the entrance and on the approach. This garden room is prettily surrounded by herb borders, shrubs in pots, and trailing creepers, which create an instantly inviting spot. From the house, however, it is concealed from view by a screening wall. A short path, densely planted, creates a sense of mystery as it leads the way to the retreat.**

should be a quality summerhouse supplier or a specialized garden home-office company. They will survey the site, advise on suitable ground support, then design and build the new building. (Some companies like to install onto a prepared concrete slab, others directly onto sunken hardwood piles.) If you are planning a garden room in tandem with building work on the house, it makes sense to employ an architect to design both jobs, to ensure visual cohesion.

A fully wired and heated garden room, once constructed, should be furnished with as much care and attention as any other room at home. Consider whether to install blinds or curtains at the windows to provide privacy and make the room cozy. Make sure, too, that you have enough storage—particularly important if you are planning to use the structure as a home office or study—and a quality floor. Wood, rubber, or matting are all excellent options. If expensive music equipment or computers are to be housed permanently, install good locks and an alarm. Many specialized garden room companies add these as standard. Given that this is a room for one person, or a few like-minded family members, inject it with plenty of personality. The interior of a modular unit may lack character, so choose to make it pretty, with a floral-upholstered daybed and cushions, or trendy, with pared-down steel and wood furniture and a cool office chair.

If you are in search of an exterior retreat but have limited outside space, consider converting an existing garage. Provided there is a driveway (or you can park on the street), the benefits of an extra room may be worth exposing your car to the elements. Many modern houses are built with internal access to the garage—useful on inclement days—and already have plumbing and lighting. If walls are exposed brick and the floor concrete, think about continuing this theme, rather than trying to disguise it, and create a robust, industrial-style workspace, with a trestle-table desk, open steel shelving, and whitewashed walls and floor.

Whatever the style of outdoor retreat, it's important that it looks good on approach. Careful, imaginative planting goes a long way to integrating the structure into the garden around it. For a traditional wooden shed, train a scented climbing plant or roses up the walls, site it beneath the natural over-hang of a bushy tree or place window boxes beneath the windows. A larger, modern structure may be flanked with rustling bamboo or tall grasses and more architectural-looking shrubs in giant galvanized pots. It can be fun to pick out the route from house to shed with flagstones set into the grass, or—if the shed or garden room is far from view—use a discreet signpost. And don't forget giant umbrellas at each door. It's cozy to sit away from the house and contemplate the sound of the rain, but only if you made it there keeping perfectly dry!

SUPPLIERS LIST

PAINT

Benjamin Moore
A wide selection of paint colors and finishes, available nationwide.
(800) 344-0400
www.benjaminmoore.com

Devine Color
A vibrant paint line that focuses on the relationships between color and light.
(866) 926-5677
www.devinecolor.com

Farrow & Ball
Muted and historical paint colors in more than 100 shades; all standard finishes plus matching exterior range.
(845) 369 4912
www.farrow-ball.com

Sherwin-Williams
Nationwide stores offer more than 1000 color choices and a large selection of wallpaper.
www.sherwinwilliams.com

WINDOW TREATMENTS

Copper Moon Woodworks
Hand-made shutters that act as sophisticated, highly visible exterior design elements.
(610) 434-8740; www.copper moonwoodworks.com

GlassWerxx
Stained-glass window shutters, oak interior shutters, and framed stained-glass panels.
(315) 493-0091
www.glasswerxx.com

Hunter Douglas
Custom-built window shadings, sheers, louvers, shades, blinds and shutters.
(800) 789-0331
www.hunterdouglas.com

Kirsch
Blinds, shades, and drapery hardware.
(800) 538-6567
www.kirsch.com

Levolor
A complete selection of shades and blinds in a variety of fabrics and styles.
(800) 538-6567
www.levolor.com

Smith & Noble
Natural romans, wood and durawood blinds, roller shades, honeycomb shade styles, panels and hardware, soft shade styles, valances and cornices, solar shades, and more.
(800) 560-0027
www.smithnoble.com

LIGHTING

Lutron
Systems to control natural daylight and electrical lighting, with dimming, switching, and shading control products.
(888) LUTRON1
www.lutron.com

Rejuvenation
Recreations of traditional American lighting and hardware.
(888) 401-1900
www.rejuvenation.com

Restoration Hardware
High-quality textiles, furniture, lighting, bathware, hardware, and amusements.
(800) 816-0901
www.restorationhardware.com

Shades of Light
Specializes in unique lamps and lighting with many original designs.
(800) 262-6612
www.shadesoflight.com

Verilux
Lighting solutions that simulate natural light, including task, ambient and direct lighting applications.
(800) 786-6850
www.healthylight.com

FIREPLACES

Crea France
Antique to contemporary fireplaces and mantels, including restoration and installation services.
(212) 213-1069
www.creafrance.com

Lennox Hearth Products
Fireplaces, freestanding stoves, fireplace inserts, and gas log sets.
www.lennoxhearthproducts.com

STORAGE

California Closets
Customized storage solutions designed for your space, available nationwide.
(888) 336-9709
www.calclosets.com

The Container Store
Helping people streamline and simplify their lives by offering an exceptional mix of storage and organization products.
(888) CONTAIN
www.containerstore.com

Hold Everything
The "Masters of Stylish Organization" feature products to make organization easy.
(800) 421-2264
www.holdeverything.com

Ikea
Large selection of affordable modular and freestanding wardrobes and storage systems.
(800) 434-4532
www.ikea.com

BATHROOMS

American Standard
The world's largest producer of bathroom and kitchen fixtures and fittings.
(800) 442-1902
www.americanstandard-us.com

Ceco
Porcelain enameled cast-iron plumbing fixtures.
(323) 588-8108
www.cecosinks.com

Clawfoot Supply
Large selection of clawfoot tubs, as well as unique and hard-to-find items such as pedestal sinks, console sinks, shower curtain rods, pull chain toilets, and curved shower rods.
(877) 682-4192
www.clawfootsupply.com

Kohler
Luxury bath products designed for gracious living.
(800) 4-KOHLER
www.kohler.com

Mansfield Plumbing Products
Attractively designed, high-performance plumbing fixtures and fittings.
(419) 938-5211
www.mansfieldplumbing.com

Sculptured Homes
Manufacturer of the WetSpa, a luxury, frameless, glass steam shower enclosure that incorporates stereo sound and fiber-optic lighting.
(877) WET-SPAS
www.sculpturedhomes.com

Waterworks
Luxury bath supplies from fixtures, fittings, and furnishings to tile, towels, and apothecary.
www.waterworks.com

SURFACES

Bisazza
Hard-wearing and sleek surfaces for bathroom worktops, walls, and sinks, in a variety of colors and finishes.
(305) 597 4099
www.bisazza.com

Corian
Long-wearing and sleek surfaces for countertops, walls, and sinks in many finishes and colors.
(800) 4-CORIAN
www.corian.com

Crossville
Porcelain stone tile, ranging from traditional styles to a line made with metals, including bronze, copper, and brass options.
(931) 484-2110
www.crossville-ceramics.com

Eco-Friendly Flooring
Wholesale supplier of environmentally friendly flooring products, including bamboo, cork, recycled glass tile, stone, and reclaimed and sustainable woods.
(866) 250-3273
www.ecofriendlyflooring.com

Junkers
Solid hardwood floors in many woods and plank widths
(714) 777-6430
www.junckershardwood.com

SileStone
Natural quartz surfaces that are heat-, scratch-, and scorch-resistant.
www.silestone.com

Vermont Soapstone
Custom manufacturer of soapstone countertops, sinks, and fireplaces.
(802) 263-5404
www.vermontsoapstone.com

PARTITIONS

Integrated Interiors
Custom-made acoustical interior solutions, including tackable wall panels, as well as home-theater systems.
(586) 756-4840
www.integratedinteriors.com

Nana Wall Systems
A full line of all glass, aluminum, clad, and wood-framed opening glass wall systems.
(800) 873-5673
www.nanawall.com

Modernfold
Operable walls and accordion partitions.
(800) 869-9685
www.modernfold.com

ATTICS

Arke Stairs
Spiral and modular stair kits.
(888) 782-4758
www.arkestairs.com

Velux
Specialists in roof windows and skylights, with a range of accessories, including blinds and window-control options.
(800) 88-VELUX
www.velux.com

GARDEN ROOMS & ACCESSORIES

Archadeck
Specializing in custom-designed and built decks, screened porches, sunrooms, gazebos and related outdoor living structures.
(800) 722-4668
www.archadeck.com

Gardener's Eden
Indoor and outdoor furnishings, tabletop, plants, and decorating accessories.
(800) 822-1214
www.gardenerseden.com

Michael Graves Pavilions
Prefabricated freestanding pavilions, designed by architect Michael Graves.
www.lindal.com/graves/

Summerwood Products
Garden sheds, storage sheds and buildings, pool cabanas, gazebos, weekend cabins, children's playhouses, and more.
(800) 663-5042
www.summerwood.com

Tanglewood Conservatories
Full-service company providing one-of-a-kind residential conservatories.
(410) 479-4700; www.tanglewoodconservatories.com

PROFESSIONAL SERVICES

Contractors.com
Free listing of contractors nationwide, with letter-graded reviews rating each contractor.
(877) 266-8722
www.contractors.com

ServiceMagic
Free service matching homeowners with architects, contractors, plumbers, and other service professionals.
(800) 474-1596
www.servicemagic.com

ARCHITECTS AND DESIGNERS

Ben Cherner, Cherner Design
T: 001 (212) 475 5656
www.chernerdesign.com

William Cummings, Heiburg
Cummings Design, T: 001 (212)
337 2030; www.hcd3.com

Patrizio Fradiani, Studio F
T: 001 (773) 880 0450
www.studiof-design.com

James Gorst T: 020 7336 7140
www.jamesgorstarchitects.com

Delphine Krakoff, Pamplemousse
Design Inc. T: 001 (212) 980 2033

Nathalie Lété, T: 00 33 (0) 1 49
60 84 76 www.nathalie-lete.com

Eric Mailaender, Resistance
Design, T: 001 (212) 714 0448
www.resistancedesign.com

James Mohn Design,
T: 001 (212) 4141477
www.jamesmohndesign.com

MOOArc Ltd, T: 01481 200021/
020 7354 1729; www.mooarc.com

Emma O'Neill at Studio Sofield Inc.
T: 001 (212) 473 1300

Ochre, T: 0870 787 9242
www.ochre.net

Dominique Picquier
T: 00 33 (0) 1 42 72 39 14
www.dominiquepicquier.com

Lena Proudlock, Berkeley House,
T: 01666 503934
www.lenaproudlock.com

Charles Rutherfoord
T: 020 7627 0182

Nicolas Vignot, T: 00 33 (0) 6 11
96 67 69, http://n.vignot.free.fr

PICTURE LOCATION CREDITS

Page 1 (half-title page), 20, 25 (top left), 28 (top left), 49 (bottom right), 50, 55, 57 (right), 72 (bottom left), 80 (top left), 114, 115 (left), 116 (left): Lena Proudlock's house in Gloucestershire, designed by Lena Proudlock.

Pages 2–3 (title pages), 14, 23 (right), 34 (top), 37, 51 (left), 52 (right), 67 (top left), 72 (top left), 138 (bottom left): Nina Gustafsson's Swedish home, designed by Nina Gustafsson.

Pages 4 (copyright page), 26 (right), 27 (left), 29, 33, 38 (left), 67 (right), 92 (bottom left), 112 (bottom left and right), 117 (right), 118, 124 (right), 131 (top right): Charles Rutherfoord and Rupert Tyler's London flat, designed by Charles Rutherfoord with Rupert Tyler.

Pages 5 (contents), 27 (right), 41, 51 (right), 69 (right), 83 (left), 87 (right), 106–7, 130, 131 (left): James Mohn and Keith Recker's apartment in New York; architecture by James Mohn and interior design as a collaboration between Keith Recker and James Mohn.

Pages 6–7, 34 (left), 49 (right, top), 52 (left), 93, 110–1, 120–1, 122–3, 126 (left), 132 (bottom), 133 (right): David Berg's house in Sweden, designed by David Berg.

Page 8: an apartment in Paris designed by Frédéric Méchiche, photograph by Andrew Wood.

Pages 9, 48–9 (main), 53, 64 (right), 74, 78 (top left), 92 (top right), 100–101, 102, 103, 126–7 (centre), 133 (left): James Falla and Lynn Graham's house in Guernsey, designed by James Falla at MOOArc.

Pages 10, 24, 56 (right), 59 (right), 67 (bottom left), 80 (top right): Harriet Maxwell Macdonald's apartment in London, designed by Harriet Maxwell Macdonald at Ochre.

Pages 11, 30–1, 32, 38 (right), 90–1, 96–7, 104, 105, 116–7 (centre), 131 (bottom right): Nathalie Lété's house in Paris, designed by Nathalie Lété.

Pages 12, 13, 62: Kristinna Ratia's Conneticut home. Photography by Andrew Wood.

Pages 15, 16–17, 44–5, 60–1, 80 (bottom), 81, 84–5, 92 (top left), 128–9, 132 (top): Patrizio Fradiani's house in Chicago, designed by Patrizio Fradiani at Studio F.

Pages 18, 19, 43, 47 (right), 58 (left), 65 (right), 112 (top), 113, 124 (bottom): a house in Suffolk designed by James Gorst.

Pages 21, 28 (right), 40, 54 (left), 58–9 (centre), 64 (left), 82, 88, 115 (right): Dominique Picquier's house in Paris, designed by Dominique Picquier.

Pages 22, 23 (left), 26 (left), 35, 42 (left), 46–7 (centre), 57 (left), 66, 73, 75, 127 (right): Reed and Delphine Krakoff's Manhattan townhouse, designed by Delphine Krakoff of Pamplemousse Design Inc.

Pages 25 (bottom right), 36, 42 (right), 68–9 (centre), 89, 94, 95: Nicolas Vignot's apartment in Paris, designed by Nicolas Vignot.

Pages 39, 54 (right), 65 (left), 86, 98, 99: Eric Mailaender's apartment in New York, designed by Eric Mailaender at Resistance Design.

Pages 46 (left), 56 (left), 83 (right), 87 (left), 124 (left): William Cumming's house on Long Island, designed by William Cummings at Heiberg Cummings Design.

Page 63: a house in New York designed by Shelton, Mindel & Associates. Photography by Andrew Wood.

Pages 70, 76–7, 78–9 (centre), 79, 108, 109, 125: Ben Cherner and Emma O'Neill's apartment in New York, designed by Emma O'Neill.

Page 71, Jasper Conran's home in London. Photography by Andrew Wood.

Pages 134–5 and 136, 137: Rachel Parnaby's home in London, designed by Rachel Parnaby.

Pages 138 (top left and right) and 139: Janine Hosegood's home in London, designed by Janine Hosegood.

Pages 140, 141: Linda Barker's house in London, designed by Linda Barker.

ACKNOWLEDGMENTS

A big thank you to Frederic, for taking such beautiful photographs, and gamely speaking English throughout the project! Thanks to all the location owners, for generously letting us into their private places. Many thanks to Jacqui Small, Kate John, Anne McDowall, and Penny Stock for their valuable editorial support, and to my agent, Fiona Lindsay, for her cheerful advice. Last, but not least, thank you to Anthony, Cicely, and Felix, who were endlessly patient while I was away shooting and always gave me the best welcome home.